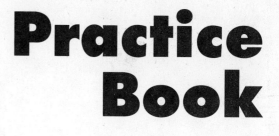

Practice Book

Grade 2

Celebrate Reading!

Scott Foresman

P9-ELW-736

ScottForesman

A Division of HarperCollinsPublishers

Editorial Offices: Glenview, Illinois
Regional Offices: Sunnyvale, California • Atlanta, Georgia
Glenview, Illinois • Oakland, New Jersey • Dallas, Texas

ISBN: 0-673-82215-X

14 15 BW 01

Table of Contents

Name _____

Theme Log

Rating Scale Rate the literature from great (1) to awful (5)

Literature	What I Learned About the Theme	How I Liked the Literature
		Great Awful
Three Up a Tree		1 2 3 4 5
There's a Hole in the Bucket		1 2 3 4 5
Jimmy Lee Did It		1 2 3 4 5
About Jimmy Lee		1 2 3 4 5
Hot Hippo		1 2 3 4 5
Rosa and Blanca		1 2 3 4 5
Additional Reading		1 2 3 4 5
		1 2 3 4 5
		1 2 3 4 5

Vocabulary

Complete the sentences below using the words from *Three Up a Tree*. Remember to use your glossary for words you are not sure about.

1. Use the words *hungry* and *listen* in a sentence about school.

_____

_____

_____

_____

2. Use the words *monster* and *snooze* in a sentence about a story.

_____

_____

_____

_____

3. Use the words *clever* and *swell* in a sentence about one of your friends.

_____

_____

_____

_____

Independent Reading Guide

Before You Read

❑ **Preview and Predict:** Look at the picture on page 6. What do you think *Three Up a Tree* is about?

_____

_____

As You Read

❑ **Pages 6-15:** Picture Lolly telling her story to Spider and Sam. Try to predict what her story will be about.

❑ **Pages 16-21:** Look at the pictures and predict what Spider's story will be about.

❑ **Pages 22-30:** Read Sam's story to find out what trick chicken and doll played on monster.

After You Read

❑ Put a check in the box if you think the story is scary, exciting, or funny. Then give each story a score. Write: Good, Very Good, or Great!

	Scary	**Exciting**	**Funny**	**Score**
Lolly's Story				
Spider's Story				
Sam's Story				

Tell which story was your favorite. Why?

_____

_____

Comprehension Check

1. Do you think the monster in Lolly's story is mean?
Explain why or why not.

_____
- -
_____
- -
_____

2. In Spider's story, how do you think the fox felt when he
looked inside the chicken's bag? Tell why you think that way.

_____
- -
_____
- -
_____

3. Why do you think this story is called *Three Up a Tree?*

_____
- -
_____
- -
_____

Predict from Previewing

Lolly, Sam, and Spider tell stories in *Three Up a Tree*. These pictures tell stories, too. Write what you predict will happen next.

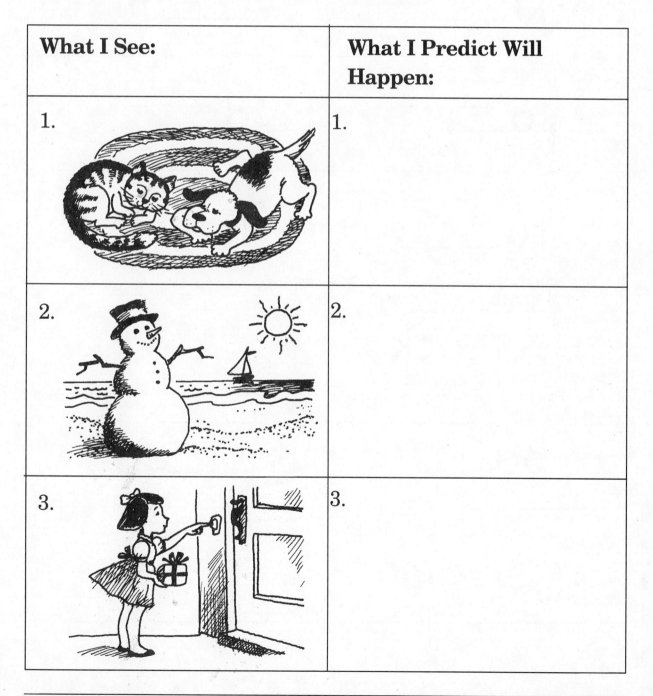

What I See:	**What I Predict Will Happen:**
1.	1.
2.	2.
3.	3.

Initial and Final Consonants

Add any letter that makes a word.
Then read your words to a friend.

1. ki _____

2. to _____

3. ru _____

4. _____ock

5. ba _____

6. _____ame

7. _____all

8. di _____

9. le _____

10. _____o

11. _____et

12. _____ide

Phonics Practice

Three Up a Tree

Initial and Final Consonants

Write the word that makes sense in each sentence.

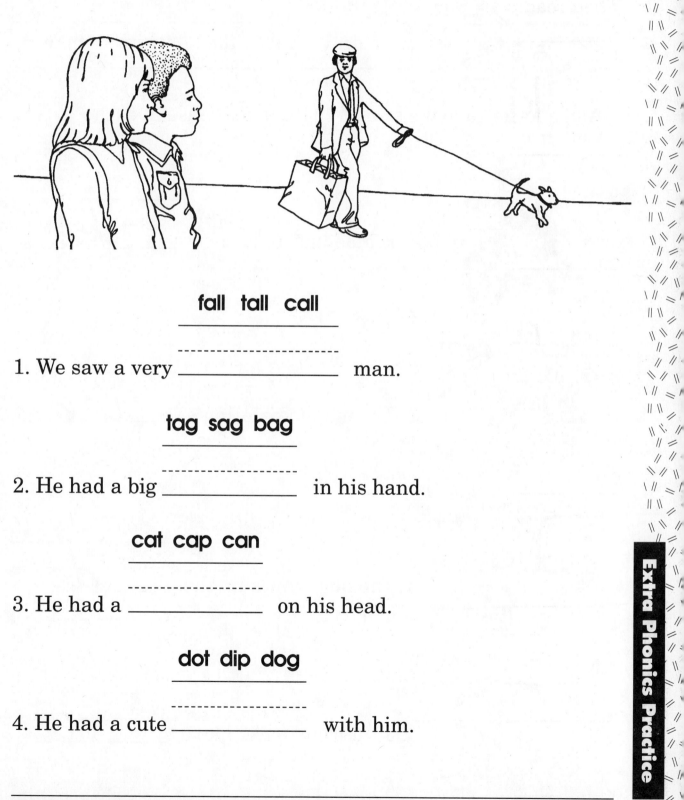

fall tall call

_____

----

1. We saw a very _____ man.

tag sag bag

_____

----

2. He had a big _____ in his hand.

cat cap can

_____

----

3. He had a _____ on his head.

dot dip dog

_____

----

4. He had a cute _____ with him.

Extra Phonics Practice

Initial Consonants

Circle the words that have the same vowel sound as *dive*.

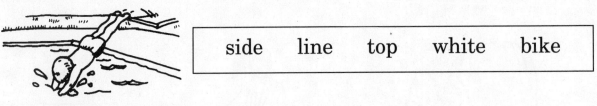

side	line	top	white	bike

Add a letter to make a word that makes sense in each sentence.

1. Emma has a nice new _____ *ike* .

2. The man is painting a _____ *ine* .

3. The bug crawls up the _____ *ide* of a tree.

4. That cloud looks like a _____ *og* .

Phonics Review

Three Up a Tree

G2

Vocabulary

These words are from *There's a Hole in the Bucket*. How much do you know about these words? Put an X below your answer.

Word	I know what this word means.	I have seen or heard this word.	I don't know what this word means.
straw			
axe			
dull			
sharpen			

Now use two of the vocabulary words you know in a sentence. Remember to check your glossary for words you are unsure about.

_____
- -
_____
- -
_____
- -
_____
- -
_____

Independent Reading Guide

Before You Read

❏ **Preview and Predict:** Read the title and look at the picture on page 33. What is the problem to be solved?

As You Read

❏ **Pages 33 to 39:** Read to find out why Henry needs to fix the bucket.

❏ **Pages 40 to 49:** Do you think Henry will ever fix the bucket?

After You Read

❏ How would you solve the problem of the bucket with a hole in it?

G2

There's a Hole in the Bucket

Comprehension Check

1. While Henry was trying to fix the bucket, what was
Liza doing?

_____

- -

_____

- -

2. If you were Liza, how would you feel at the end of the story?
Explain.

_____

- -

_____

- -

_____

3. Henry never did fix the bucket! Why not? Explain.

_____

- -

_____

- -

_____

Sequence: Order of Events

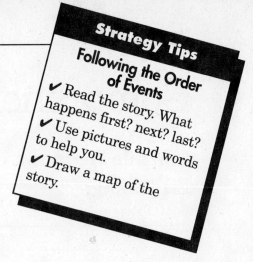

Draw something that happened in *There's a Hole in the Bucket*. Write a sentence to go with your picture. Look at the pictures your classmates drew and put them in order.

There's a Hole in the Bucket

G2

Short Vowel Sounds

Use the words in the box. Label the pictures.

sun sack hat duck pig well rock

There's a Hole in the Bucket

Phonics Practice

Name _____

Short Vowel Sounds

Use the words in the box. Write the word that makes sense in each sentence.

fun sat fish went frog bed

1. My friend and I _____ to a pond today.

2. We had so much _____ !

3. We could see many _____ in the water.

4. We saw a _____ jump into the water.

5. We _____ by the pond and watched for a long time.

There's a Hole in the Bucket

G2

Final Consonants

Write *ll* under each picture whose
name ends like *shell*.

she**ll**

1. dre_____	2. be_____	3. cra_____
4. do_____	5. ba_____	6. sme_____

Write the word that makes sense in each sentence.

fall   will

7. The girl _____ help Mom.

ball   tell

8. The girl finds a _____ .

Using a Table of Contents

Contents

1. On which page in the book would you find "Communities"?

_____

_____

2. Which lesson is located on page 34?

_____

_____

3. In which unit do you find "Family Celebrations"?

_____

_____

There's a Hole in the Bucket

G2

Study Skills

Vocabulary

The following questions include words that you will find in *Jimmy Lee Did It*. You may need to use your glossary to answer these questions.

1. Have you ever taken the *blame* for something? What happened?

_____

_____

2. How would you *describe* yourself?

_____

_____

3. What *remains* a *mystery* to you?

_____

_____

4. Ask a question using each of these words. Use your glossary for help.

capture

_____

_____

trace

_____

_____

Independent Reading Guide

Before You Read

❑ **Preview and Predict:** Read the title and page 57. What did Jimmy Lee do? What else will he do?

As You Read

❑ **Pages 57 to 61:** Find out what Jimmy Lee does to Artie and Angel. Was your prediction correct?

❑ **Pages 62 to 67:** How would you tell Angel to catch Jimmy Lee?

❑ **Pages 68 to 72:** Who is Jimmy Lee?

After You Read

❑ Design a Jimmy Lee "Catcher." Draw or write about a plan to catch Jimmy Lee.

Jimmy Lee Did It

Comprehension Check

Draw a picture that shows what Jimmy Lee does at Angel's house. Then tell why you think he never gets caught.

Predict from Previewing

Strategy Tips

Predicting

✔ Look at the pictures. What do you see?

✔ Ask questions about the pictures. What do you wonder?

Choose a book you haven't read. Write down the name of the story, what you see in the pictures and what you wonder will happen.

Story	What I See	What I Wonder

Jimmy Lee Did It

G2

Long Vowel Sounds

Use the words in the box to complete the poem.
Then draw a picture about it.

| bone | cake | hole | rice | mine | Jake | ate |

_____

Stop it, _____! This isn't nice!

You made a hole and spilled the _____!

You nibbled chicken off the _____!

You ate the side of my corn pone!

You chewed a _____ in my

birthday _____!

And _____ my rose,

for goodness sake!

Jake, I know this food tastes fine,

But you're a hamster!

This food's _____!

Phonics Practice

Long Vowel Sounds

Say the name of each picture. Circle the word that has the same vowel sound.

1. cab   trap   bake

2. shell   cone   hog

3. shop   sill   hive

4. pen   feet   bell

5. tug   June   net

6. beg   fade   sash

Extra Phonics Practice

Jimmy Lee Did It

Short Vowels

Write the word that makes sense in each sentence.

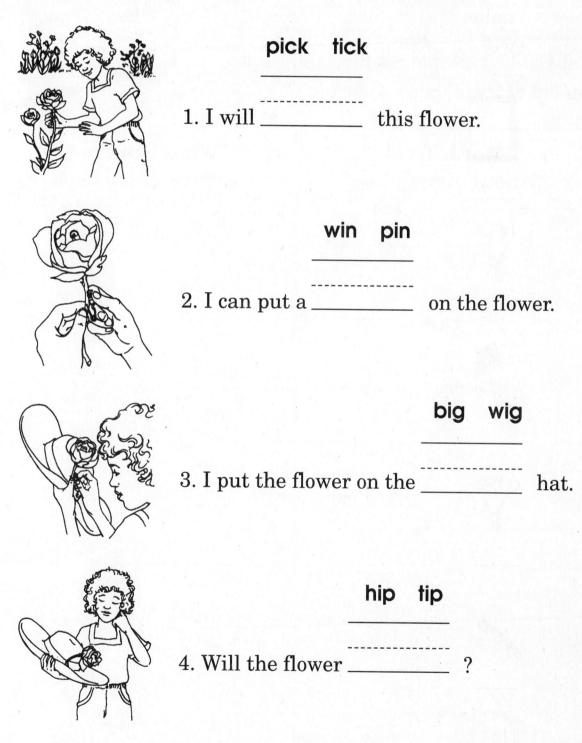

pick   tick

_____

- - - - - - - - - - - -

1. I will _____ this flower.

win   pin

_____

- - - - - - - - - - - -

2. I can put a _____ on the flower.

big   wig

_____

- - - - - - - - - - - -

3. I put the flower on the _____ hat.

hip   tip

_____

- - - - - - - - - - - -

4. Will the flower _____ ?

Phonics Review

Use Context: Unfamiliar Words

Write down words in "About Jimmy Lee" that you had trouble reading. Tell what you did to try to figure them out.

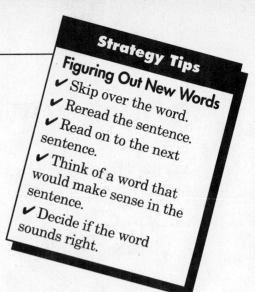

Strategy Tips

Figuring Out New Words
- ✔ Skip over the word.
- ✔ Reread the sentence.
- ✔ Read on to the next sentence.
- ✔ Think of a word that would make sense in the sentence.
- ✔ Decide if the word sounds right.

Words from "About Jimmy Lee"	What I Did to Figure Them Out

G2

About Jimmy Lee

Single Final Vowels

Use the letters in the box.
Write the last letter of each word.

y	e	o

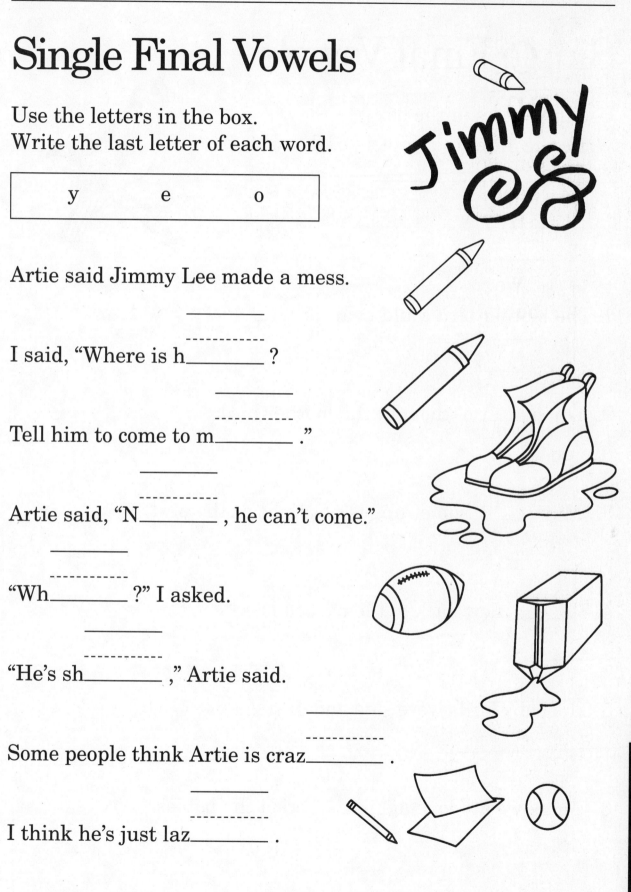

Artie said Jimmy Lee made a mess.

‾‾‾‾‾‾‾‾

I said, "Where is h_____ ?

‾‾‾‾‾‾‾‾

Tell him to come to m_____ ."

‾‾‾‾‾‾‾‾

Artie said, "N_____ , he can't come."

‾‾‾‾‾‾‾‾

"Wh_____ ?" I asked.

‾‾‾‾‾‾‾‾

"He's sh_____ ," Artie said.

‾‾‾‾‾‾‾‾

Some people think Artie is craz_____ .

‾‾‾‾‾‾‾‾

I think he's just laz_____ .

Phonics Practice

Single Final Vowels

Use the letters in the box.
Write the letter to complete each word.

y	e	o

1. The mother bird could hear a cr_____ .

2. "Oh, n_____ ," thought the mother bird.

3. "Mayb_____ something is not right at the nest."

4. Sh_____ flew back to the nest to look.

5. The baby birds were safe and dr_____ .

6. "Mom, we ate long ag_____ ," cried the babies.

7. "W_____ are hungry!"

About Jimmy Lee

Extra Phonics Practice

Final Blend -nd

Write *nd* under each picture
whose name ends like *band*.

ba**nd**

_____ --------- 1. po_____	_____ --------- 2. gi_____	_____ --------- 3. ha_____
_____ --------- 4. ne_____	_____ --------- 5. sa_____	_____ --------- 6. wi_____

Write a word from above to complete each sentence.

7. The ducks took a swim in the _____ .

8. The _____ blew off my hat.

Phonics Review

Folk Tales

Complete after reading *Hot Hippo* and *Rosa and Blanca.*

In folk tales, animals sometimes act like people. What things does Hot Hippo do that people also do?

_____

- -

_____

- -

_____

In folk tales some characters do good things. What good things do Rosa and Blanca do?

_____

- -

_____

- -

_____

- -

_____

Try one of these ideas:

- Folk tales are often told or read aloud. Retell to a partner a story someone has told to you. You might want to write down what you plan to say.
- Find a folk tale picture book in the library. Read the story to yourself and then retell it to a friend, showing the pictures as you retell the story from memory.

Genre Study

Hot Hippo

Vocabulary

Use any of the words below to finish the sentences.

agreed   bank   gazed   hopefully   mountain

The young boy

_____

- - - - - - - - - - - - - - - - - -

_____

- - - - - - - - - - - - - - - - - -

_____

- - - - - - - - - - - - - - - - - -

_____

Today I am

_____

- - - - - - - - - - - - - - - - - -

_____

- - - - - - - - - - - - - - - - - -

_____

- - - - - - - - - - - - - - - - - -

_____

Independent Reading Guide

Before You Read

❏ **Preview and Predict:** Look at the picture on pages 88-89. There is a thought bubble coming from Hippo. What might he be thinking?

As You Read

❏ **Pages 88 to 93:** Find out why Hippo doesn't jump into the water.

❏ **Pages 94 to 102:** Read to find out if Hippo gets his wish to live in the water.

After You Read

❏ Draw your favorite part of the story. Write down why you liked this part best.

Comprehension Check

1. If Ngai didn't let Hippo live in the water, how do you think Hippo would feel? Explain why you think that way.

_____
- -
_____
- -
_____

2. Oh no, Hippo can't swim! Does it matter? Explain.

_____
- -
_____
- -
_____

3. Do you think Hippo will keep his promise? Explain your thinking.

_____
- -
_____
- -
_____

Sequence: Order of Events

Put events in *Hot Hippo* in order. Write what happened in the beginning, in the middle, and at the end. Draw a picture to go with each sentence.

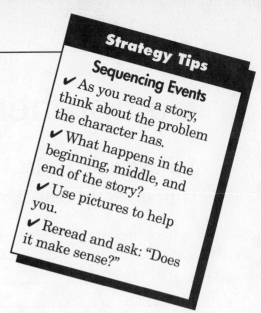

When?	What Happens?	Draw a Picture.
Beginning		
Middle		
End		

Hot Hippo

Medial Consonants

Answer these riddles by writing the missing letters.

1. What is a baby cat called?

ki _ _ _ en

2. What animal has orange and black stripes?

ti _ _ er

3. What animal has one or two humps on its back?

ca _ _ el

4. What furry animal hops around?

ra _ _ _ it

5. What is a baby dog called?

pu _ _ _ y

6. What has eight legs and spins a web?

spi _ _ er

Make up your own animal riddle.

_____

_____

_____

Medial Consonants

Look at the pictures and words in the box. Write the missing letters for the word that answers each question.

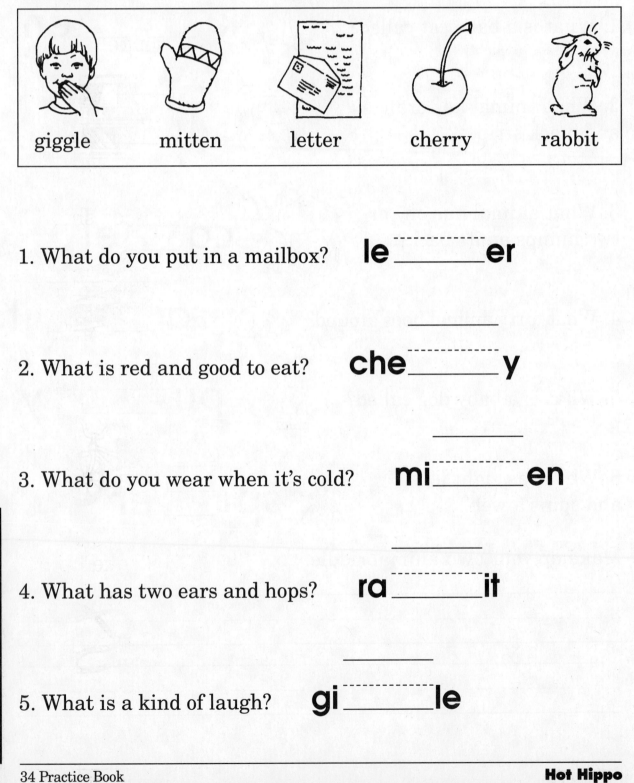

giggle   mitten   letter   cherry   rabbit

1. What do you put in a mailbox?   le _____ er

2. What is red and good to eat?   che _____ y

3. What do you wear when it's cold?   mi _____ en

4. What has two ears and hops?   ra _____ it

5. What is a kind of laugh?   gi _____ le

Long Vowels

Name each picture. Listen to its vowel sound. Circle the word above the picture that has the same vowel sound.

1. kitten   slide

2. call   lake

3. spoke   hook

4. rule   nut

5. like   slid

6. bake   shine

7. name   trap

8. hoop   joke

9. vine   bin

10. will   bride

11. huge   tub

12. smoke   spot

Phonics Review

Hot Hippo

Vocabulary

These words can describe a meal. Use the words to write sentences about a meal. Use your glossary if you need help.

chiles

_____

- -

half

_____

- -

passed

_____

- -

tomatoes

_____

- -

tortilla

_____

- -

Write a sentence about a meal. Use at least one of the words above in your sentence.

_____

- -

_____

- -

Rosa and Blanca

G2

Independent Reading Guide

Before You Read

❑ **Preview and Predict:** Look at the picture on pages 104 and 105. Who, do you think, are Rosa and Blanca?

As You Read

❑ **Pages 104–109:** Find out why Rosa and Blanca decide to share the food from their gardens.

❑ **Pages 110–113:** How was the mystery of the extra tomatoes, corn, and chiles solved?

TIP!

☞ Notice as you read about the mystery of the extra vegetables, that the same thing happens three times.

After You Read

❑ Choose a partner. Talk about how you felt after reading the story of Rosa and Blanca. Make a list of things you and your partner can do to help others.

How We Can Help Others

_____

- - - - - - - - - - - - - - - - - - - -

_____

- - - - - - - - - - - - - - - - - - - -

_____

- - - - - - - - - - - - - - - - - - - -

_____

- - - - - - - - - - - - - - - - - - - -

_____

- - - - - - - - - - - - - - - - - - - -

_____

Comprehension Check

Draw a picture that shows how Rosa and Blanca help each
other in the story. Then tell why you think they help each other
so much.

Rosa and Blanca

G2

Use Context: Unfamiliar Words

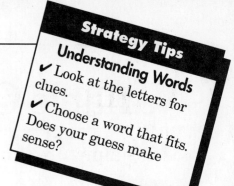

Read each sentence from *Rosa and Blanca*.
Say the bold words out loud. What do they mean?

Sentence	What Word Means
"Rosa added her tomatoes to the pile in Blanca's **kitchen**." (p. 108) "She picked him up and **rocked** him." (p. 111)	

Variable Consonant Sounds of c and g

Circle the words that have a **c** or a **g**.

At the parade, we saw boys and girls with painted faces,

huge bears that danced in a car, and

a giant that gave away funny caps.

Write the words you circled in the correct list below.

Words with c as in cup
_____
- -
_____
- -
_____

Words with c as in city
_____
- -
_____
- -
_____

Words with g as in gate
_____
- -
_____
- -
_____

Words with g as in giraffe
_____
- -
_____
- -
_____

Phonics Practice

Rosa and Blanca

G2

Variable Consonant Sounds of c and g

Use the words in the box. Write the word that makes sense in each sentence.

| pencil | circle | nice | giant | page | age |

1. Joan wrote a story about a

   _____

   big, noisy _____ .

2. He is the same _____ as Joan.

3. She uses a _____ to draw his picture.

4. She makes a round _____ for his mouth.

5. Joan thinks he would be

   _____

   a _____ friend to have.

Extra Phonics Practice

Single Final Vowels

Use the words in the box. Write the word that makes sense in each sentence.

Maybe	cry	be	very	me	go

1. The thrush looks _____ tiny in the nest.

2. It can _____ a hard bird to find.

3. The _____ of the owl makes the thrush hide.

4. "My noise makes the thrush _____ away," says Woodpecker.

5. "_____ the thrush will visit me," says Bill.

Phonics Review

G2

Theme Log

Name _____

Rating Scale   (1) deserves an award   (1)⊘ does not deserve award

Literature	What I Learned About the Theme	How I Liked the Literature
Regina's Big Mistake		(1) (1)⊘
Totem Pole Boy		(1) (1)⊘
Emma's Dragon Hunt		(1) (1)⊘
Giants/The Chicken and the Egg		(1) (1)⊘
The Story		(1) (1)⊘
Eddy B, Pigboy		(1) (1)⊘
For the Birds		(1) (1)⊘
Additional Reading		(1) (1)⊘
		(1) (1)⊘

Vocabulary

Write sentences using the words from *Regina's Big Mistake*.
Remember to use your glossary for words you
are not sure about.

1. Use the words *crumpled* and *mistake* in a sentence
about a drawing.

_____

- -

_____

2. Use the words *concentrating* and *copycat* in a sentence
about two students.

_____

- -

_____

3. Use the words *invisible* and *jungle* in a sentence about
an animal.

_____

- -

_____

4. Use the words *rain forest* and *sprouted* in a sentence
about plants.

_____

- -

_____

Regina's Big Mistake

Independent Reading Guide

Before You Read

❏ **Preview and Predict:** Read the title and look at the pictures. Where does the story take place?

As You Read

❏ **Pages 8 to 23:** Read to find out what problems Regina has with Mrs. Li's assignment. What is Regina's first mistake? What is her second mistake?

❏ **Pages 24 to 28:** Can Regina fix her mistakes and finish Mrs. Li's assignment? Read on to find out what happens.

After You Read

❏ Use your imagination and finish the drawing below.

Comprehension Check

1. How does Regina feel when she makes a mistake?
Explain how you know.

_____

_____
_____

_____

2. Stuart and Nathalie both thought Regina was trying
to copy their pictures. Do you think she was? Tell why
you think that way.

_____

_____
_____

_____

3. Imagine that Regina had not made a mistake when
she drew her sun. Do you think her picture would have been
better, or not as good? Explain.

_____

_____
_____

_____

Regina's Big Mistake

© Scott, Foresman and Company   G2

Cause and Effect

Draw a picture of something that
happened in *Regina's Big Mistake*.
Then draw another picture to show what
happened after that.

Compound Words

Find and circle seven compound words.
Draw a line between each part like this: space/ship
Finish the story.

I was inside when the
spaceship landed in
my backyard.

A monster with an eye as big
as a football came out. He had
a hairy eyebrow.

He came to the doorstep and
rang the doorbell.

Here's what happened.

_____

- -

_____

- -

_____

- -

_____

Phonics Practice

Regina's Big Mistake

G2

Compound Words

Add a word from the box to a word below to make a new word.

| coat   blue   house |
| walk   any |

1. rain _____

2. side _____

3. _____ bird

4. _____ time

5. tree _____

| sun   dog   room |
| boat   book |

6. sail _____

7. _____ house

8. bed _____

9. _____ shine

10. note _____

Extra Phonics Practice

Short Vowel Sounds

Name each picture. Listen to its vowel sound. Circle the word that has the same vowel sound.

	1.	cane	trap	hip
	2.	size	beak	jet
	3.	fig	tide	dime
	4.	poke	thin	spot
	5.	blame	nut	June
	6.	wade	peg	flap

Phonics Review

Regina's Big Mistake

Using a Glossary

Glossary _____

airplane a flying machine driven by propellers or jet engines. *I like to travel by airplane.* **airplanes.**

because for the reason that; since: *Mom called us because supper was ready.*

bird an animal that has wings and feathers: *Most birds can fly.* **birds.**

birthday the day on which a person was born. *My birthday is on July 4th.* **birthdays.**

can't cannot.

catch 1. take and hold something that is moving: *Try to catch the ball in the air.* **caught, catching. 2.** the act of catching: *She made a good catch in the ball game.* **catches.**

child a young boy or girl: *The girl is our neighbor's child.* **children.**

class a group of pupils taught together. **classes.**

climb go up something too steep to walk up: *I will climb the tree.* **climbed, climbing.**

come 1. move toward: *Come over to me.* 2. get near; reach; arrive: *The girls will come home tomorrow.* **came, coming.**

could was able; was able to: *She could swim.*

1. What should the first guide word be?

_____

_____

2. What is the definition of *because?*

_____

_____

3. Between which two words would you put *clever?*

_____

_____

Vocabulary

The following questions include words that you will find in *Totem Pole Boy* and the poems that come before it. You may need to use your glossary to answer these questions.

1. What do *members* of a *tribe* have in common?

_____

- -

_____

2. Is *dusk* in the morning or in the evening?

_____

- -

_____

3. What kinds of things do people *carve?*

_____

- -

_____

4. Ask a question using each of these words. Use your glossary for help.

billows

_____

- -

_____

pollen

_____

- -

_____

Independent Reading Guide

Before You Read

❏ **Preview and Predict:**
Read the title and look at the pictures. Is this story make-believe or about real people?

As You Read

❏ **Pages 36 to 38:** Read to find out what David and his father must do to find a perfect tree and carve a totem pole.

After You Read

❏ The totem pole in the picture tells about someone your age. What can you learn about the person from the totem pole?

_____

_____

_____

_____

Comprehension Check

1. Draw a picture that shows what David's father does.

2. Do you think *Totem Pole Boy* is a good name for this article?
Tell why or why not.

_____

_____

_____

_____

3. Do you think David will want to carve totem poles someday?
Tell why you think that way.

_____

_____

_____

_____

Reread and Read on

Fill in each column with information from
Totem Pole Boy.

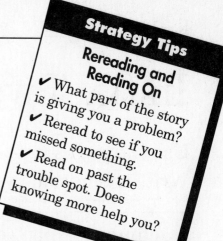

Strategy Tips

Rereading and Reading On
✔ What part of the story is giving you a problem?
✔ Reread to see if you missed something.
✔ Read on past the trouble spot. Does knowing more help you?

Identify Trouble Spot	Reread to Understand	Read On to Understand

Initial Two-Letter Blends

Use the words in the box.
Write the missing words to complete the story.

| climbed | played | dragon | tricks | sleeping | dream |

I was _____ when

a _____ came into my room.

I _____ onto his back.

I taught him _____ .

We _____ for hours.
Then I woke up.

It was only a _____ .

Phonics Practice

Totem Pole Boy

© Scott, Foresman and Company   G2

Initial Two-Letter Blends

Say the name of each picture. Write the letters that stand for the beginning sounds.

cl	dr	fl	fr	sl	st	sw	tr

1. _____

2. _____

3. _____

4. _____

5. _____

6. _____

7. _____

8. _____

9. _____

Extra Phonics Practice

Totem Pole Boy

Variable Sounds of c and g

Use the words in the box. Write the words to complete the story.

| exercise | large | city | village | bicycle | germ |

1. Carol likes to ride her

   _____

   - - - - - - - - - - - - - - - - - - -

   _____ every day.

2. Saturday, Carol will ride her

   _____

   - - - - - - - - - - - - - - - - -

   bike to a _____ .

3. She has to ride through a _____
   to get to the country.

4. Carol likes to ride up the

   _____

   - - - - - - - - - - - - - - - - -

   _____ hills.

5. Riding a bike is a great way

   _____

   - - - - - - - - - - - - - - -

   to get _____ .

Totem Pole Boy

Visualizing

Look for details in *Emma's Dragon Hunt* to help you picture the dragons.

Weather Event	Details Found	How I Picture the Dragons
Thunderstorm		
Rainbow		

Final Two-Letter Blends

Use the letters in the box.
Write the missing letters in the poem.

rt	st	nd

Dragon Guest

A dragon guest can be a pest _____
                              - - - - - - - - - - - -

Unless, as host, you do your be _____

To serve the beast a feast of roast _____   _____
                                    - - - - - - - -   - - - - - - - -

And for desse _____ , a mou _____ of toast.
              - - - - - - -   - - - - - - -

Then give your gue _____ some time to re _____ ;
                   - - - - - - -   - - - - - - -

Suggest he let his food digest. _____
                                - - - - - - -

And while he rests, just tiptoe pa _____ ,
                                   - - - - - -

Or this guest pe _____ will be your last.
                 - - - - - -

Phonics Practice

Emma's Dragon Hunt

Final Two-Letter Blends

Say each word. Circle the letters that stand for the ending sounds. Complete the word that makes sense in each sentence.

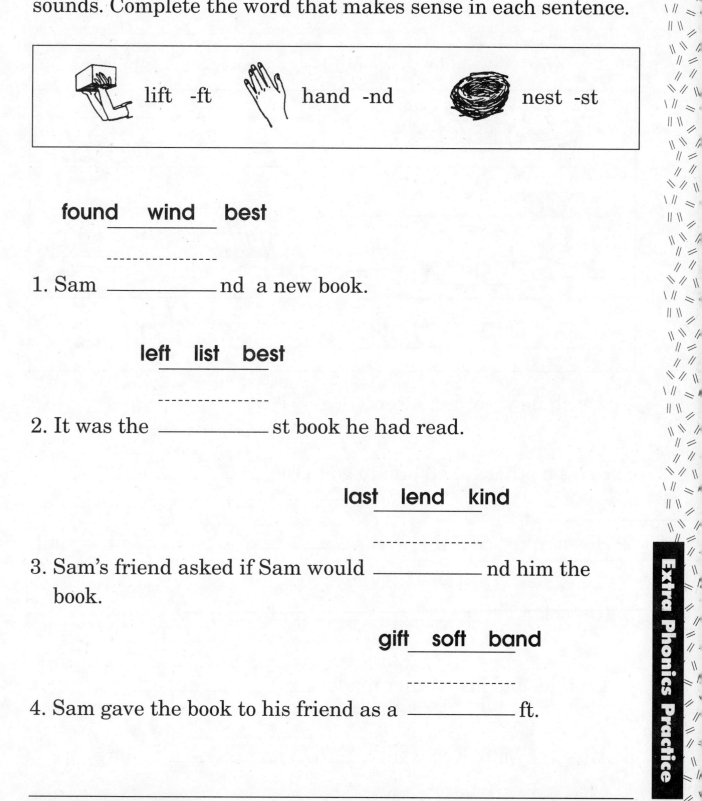

lift -ft   hand -nd   nest -st

found   wind   best

----

1. Sam _____ nd a new book.

left   list   best

----

2. It was the _____ st book he had read.

last   lend   kind

----

3. Sam's friend asked if Sam would _____ nd him the book.

gift   soft   band

----

4. Sam gave the book to his friend as a _____ ft.

Extra Phonics Practice

Compound Words

Use the words in the box. Add a word to each word below to make a compound word.

any	side	mail	corn	short

_____ _____ *cut*

pop _____ _____ *out*

_____ *box* _____ *thing*

Use each new word in a sentence.

_____

1. Ken's mother asked him to go to the _____ .

_____

2. He went to see if there was _____ in the mail.

_____

3. He took a _____ and was home soon.

_____

4. Then he and his mother made _____ .

_____

5. After they ate, Ken went _____ to play.

Emma's Dragon Hunt

Play

Complete after reading *Giants* and *The Chicken and the Egg*.

Stage directions in plays tell what the actors do or how they act their parts. Name some things the children in *Giants* do to make themselves look big.

_____

- -
_____

_____

- -
_____

The dark type in a play tells who is speaking. Use the dark type to find out which characters sing the song first in *The Chicken and the Egg*. Which sing second?

_____

- -
_____

_____

- -
_____

Try one of these ideas:

- Plays can be practiced before doing them for others. Think of a story that would make a good play. Talk with a friend about the characters, the setting, and the costumes you would need for this play.

- Make a puppet of a character from a play. Make the props the character will need in the play and practice with friends who have made other puppets from the same play.

Genre Study

Vocabulary

Write sentences below using words from *Giants* and *The Chicken and the Egg*. Remember to use your glossary for words you are not sure about.

1. Use the words *clenching* and *shrinking* in a sentence about people acting.

_____

_____

_____

2. Use the words *giants, normal,* and *doubt* in a sentence about size.

_____

_____

_____

3. Use the words *cast* and *costumes* in a sentence about a play.

_____

_____

_____

Giants/The Chicken and the Egg

Independent Reading Guide

Before You Read

❏ **Preview and Predict:** Read the titles and look at the pictures and text. How are *Giants* and *The Chicken and the Egg* different from other stories?

As You Read

❏ **Pages 66 to 68:** Read to find out how the children in the play make themselves look like giants.

TIP!

When you read a play, the dark type tells you who is speaking.

❏ **Pages 69 to 73:** Will the children be able to fool the real giant? Read on to find out their secret plan.

❏ **Pages 74 to 80:** Read to find out what problem has everyone quarreling and cackling.

After You Read

❏ Settle the argument between the chicken and the egg. Which do you think came first? Why?

_____

- -

_____

- -

_____

- -

_____

- -

_____

Giants/The Chicken and the Egg

Comprehension Check

Giants

1. Draw a picture that shows how you would make yourself look like a giant.

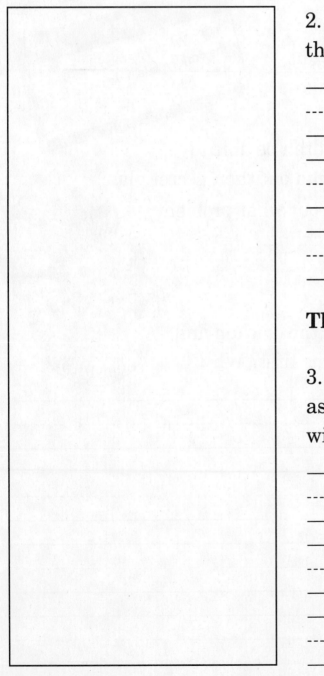

2. Do you think the giant in the play is smart? Explain.

The Chicken and the Egg

3. If the chickens and eggs ask *you* who comes first, what will you say?

Giants/The Chicken and the Egg

Name _____

Using Text Features

Read the stage directions from *Giants*.
Draw a picture of what is happening. Write
the stage directions at the bottom of your
picture.

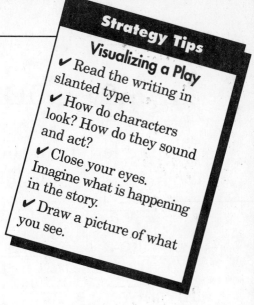

*The giant falls asleep. He puts his
face in his hands and closes his eyes.*

© Scott, Foresman and Company   G2

Initial Consonant Digraphs

Use the letters in the box.
Write the missing letters in the words.

| wh | sh | ch | th |

If you were a giant, you could

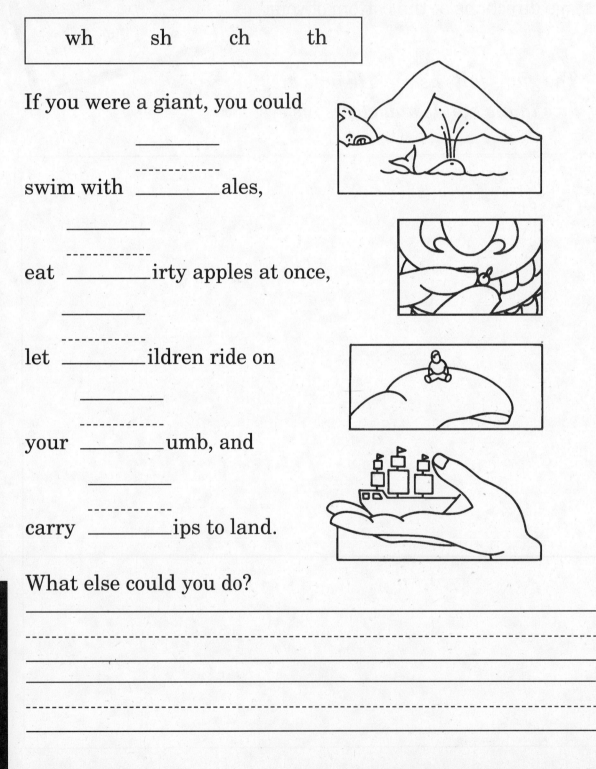

swim with _____ales,

eat _____irty apples at once,

let _____ildren ride on

your _____umb, and

carry _____ips to land.

What else could you do?

_____
_____
_____
_____
_____

Giants/The Chicken and the Egg

© Scott, Foresman and Company   G2

Initial Consonant Digraphs

Use the words in the box. Write the word that makes sense in each sentence.

children   thought   thank   when   show

1. The queen heard music
_____
- - - - - - - - - - - - - - - - - - -
_____ she went for a walk.

_____
- -
2. She _____ the
sound came from the garden.

3. She found her family putting on a
_____
- - - - - - - - - - - - - - -
_____ .

_____
- -
4. The _____ sang
and played.

5. The queen hugged her children
_____
- - - - - - - - - - - - - - - - - - -
to _____ them.

Giants/The Chicken and the Egg

Initial Blends

Say the name of each picture. Write the letters that stand for the beginning sound.

bl	cl	fl	sl	gl	pl

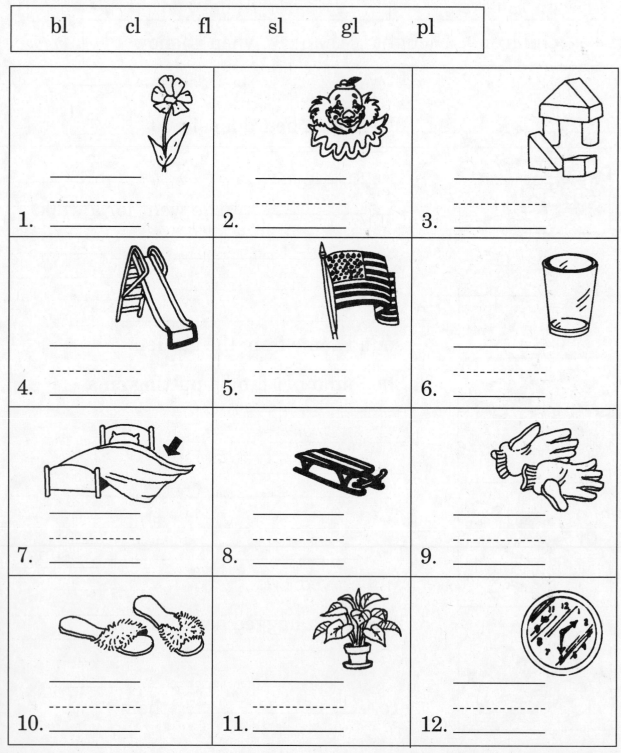

1. _____

2. _____

3. _____

4. _____

5. _____

6. _____

7. _____

8. _____

9. _____

10. _____

11. _____

12. _____

Giants/The Chicken and the Egg

© Scott, Foresman and Company   G2

Vocabulary

Use the words below in sentences about the pictures.

bang   built   poured   sandcastles   tilt   wept

The girl

_____

- -

_____

- -

_____

- -

_____

Later that day

_____

- -

_____

- -

_____

- -

_____

Independent Reading Guide

Before You Read

❏ **Preview and Predict:** What kind of characters are Frog and Toad? What words could describe them?

As You Read

❏ **Pages 82 to 86:** Read to find out why Frog is in bed. What favor does Frog ask from Toad?

TIP!
☞ Find out the differences between a frog and a toad.

❏ **Pages 87 to 89:** Does Toad do the favor for Frog? Read to find out who tells the story and what the story is about.

After You Read

❏ Finish this story about Frog and Toad.

Two good friends named Frog and Toad
went for a walk down a country road.

The Story

G2

Comprehension Check

1. Why do you think Toad starts feeling sick?

_____

- -

_____

- -

_____

2. How does Frog think of a story to tell Toad?

_____

- -

_____

- -

_____

3. How do you think Frog and Toad feel about each other?
Explain why you think that way.

_____

- -

_____

- -

_____

Finding the Main Idea

Find the supporting ideas and main idea
in one of the Pigericks.

Strategy Tips

Finding the Main Idea
✔ The main idea tells the
most important idea in
the story.
✔ Think about the things
the character does.
✔ Think about the most
important idea in the
story.

What Does the Pig Do?	What is the Main Idea?

The Story

Final Consonant Digraphs

Say the name of each picture. Write the letters that stand for the ending sound.

-ch   -ng   -sh   -th

1. tee_____

2. bru_____

3. spla_____

4. bea_____

5. di_____

6. ri_____

7. pea_____

8. swi_____

9. fi_____

The Story

Final Blends

Circle the word to complete each sentence.

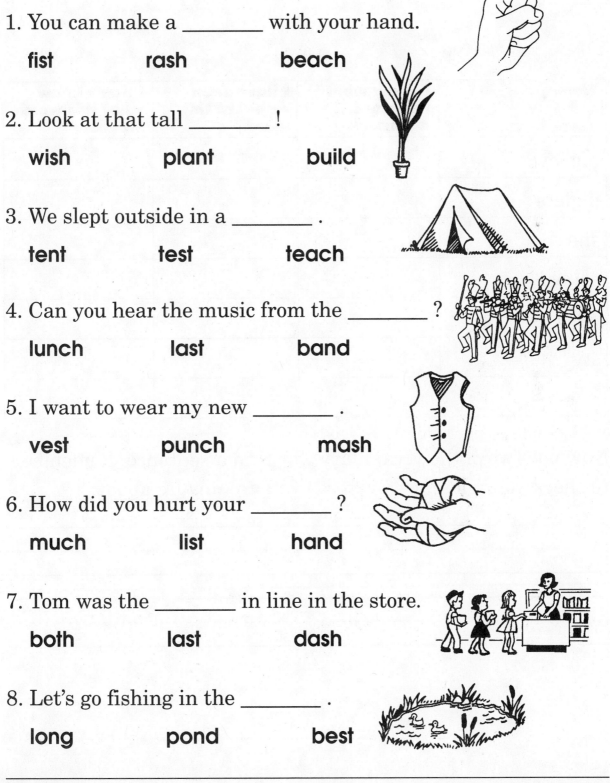

1. You can make a _____ with your hand.

   fist   rash   beach

2. Look at that tall _____!

   wish   plant   build

3. We slept outside in a _____.

   tent   test   teach

4. Can you hear the music from the _____?

   lunch   last   band

5. I want to wear my new _____.

   vest   punch   mash

6. How did you hurt your _____?

   much   list   hand

7. Tom was the _____ in line in the store.

   both   last   dash

8. Let's go fishing in the _____.

   long   pond   best

The Story

Phonics Review

Vocabulary

These words are from *Eddy B, Pigboy*. How much do you know about these words? Put an X below your answer.

Word	I know what this word means.	I have seen or heard this word.	I don't know what this word means.
pigboy			
piglets			
sneak			
squeal			
pigsty			
sty			
nurse			

Now use two of the vocabulary words in a sentence. Remember to check your glossary for words you are unsure about.

_____

- -

_____

- -

_____

G2

Independent Reading Guide

Before You Read

❏ **Preview and Predict:** Where does the story take place? Why is Eddy called a Pigboy?

As You Read

❏ **Pages 98 to 105:** Read to find out what Eddy B's job is as pigboy on his family's farm.

❏ **Pages 106 to 108:** What happens to the mama pig and her piglets after Eddy B brings them home? What happens to Eddy B after his job is done?

After You Read

❏ Tell if you would like to exchange places with Eddy B for one day. Explain why.

_____

Eddy B, Pigboy

Comprehension Check

1. Be Daisy D. Tell what you see when Eddy B brings home the pigs.

_____

- -

_____

- -

_____

2. Do you think Eddy B likes his job? Explain why you think that way.

_____

- -

_____

- -

_____

3. Would you like to be a pigboy or piggirl? Tell why or why not.

_____

- -

_____

- -

_____

Eddy B, Pigboy

Cause and Effect

Fill in the story chain. Tell what happens in
Eddy B, Pigboy.

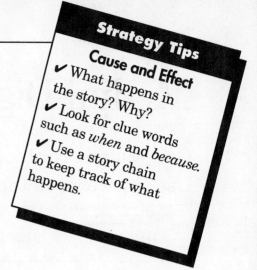

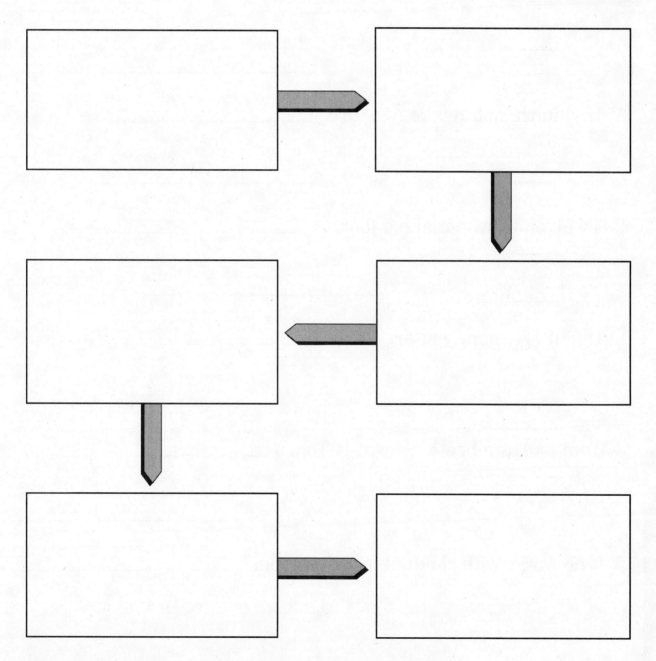

You may continue the story on your own paper.

Medial Digraphs and Blends

Can you answer these riddles?
Use the words in the box and write the answers.

| inches | asleep | teacher | sister | angry |

1. If you are not awake, you are _____ _____ .

2. Twelve of these make a foot. _____ _____

3. If you are mad, you are _____ _____ .

4. Tom is Ann's brother. Ann is Tom's _____ _____ .

5. Who works with children in a classroom? _____ _____

© Scott, Foresman and Company   G2

Phonics Practice

Eddy B, Pigboy

Medial Digraphs and Blends

Read the first word. Circle the other word or words
with the same middle sound.

1. air<u>cr</u>aft	airplane	across	secret
2. chil<u>dr</u>en	hundred	chilly	laundry
3. pur<u>ch</u>ase	recall	exchange	purple
4. some<u>th</u>ing	bathtub	author	nothing
5. in<u>cl</u>ude	exclaim	enclose	reply

Eddy B, Pigboy

Initial Consonant Digraphs

Use the letters in the box. Write the letters that begin each word.

ch	sh	th	wh

1. _____

2. _____

3. _____

4. _____

5. _____

6. _____

7. _____

8. _____

9. _____

10. _____

11. _____

12. _____

Eddy B, Pigboy

Vocabulary

The following questions include words that you will find in *For the Birds*. You may need to use your glossary to answer these questions.

1. What kind of creature *fluffs* itself up?

_____

_____

_____

2. Does a person use more *energy* to run or to sit?

_____

_____

_____

3. What can grow in *ceramic* pots?

_____

_____

_____

4. Ask a question using each of these words. Use your glossary for help.

saucer

_____

_____

metal

_____

_____

Name _____

Independent Reading Guide

Before You Read

❏ **Preview and Predict:** Read the title and look at the pictures. What is this story about?

As You Read

❏ **Pages 112 to 113:** Find out why birds are attracted to yards with birdbaths. Write down one interesting fact you read about birds.

❏ **Pages 114 to 116:** Read about how to make a bird feeder and a birdbath.

After You Read

❏ Design a birdhouse for sparrows. Use the space below for your drawing.

Comprehension Check

1. Do you think *For the Birds* is a good title for this article? Tell why you think that way.

_____

- -

_____

- -

_____

2. Could you make a birdbath out of a soup can? Explain why or why not.

_____

- -

_____

- -

_____

3. Tell how you would like to help birds.

_____

- -

_____

- -

Main Idea and Supporting Details

Find the main idea and supporting details on page 116 of *For the Birds*.

Main Idea	Details

Initial Three-Letter Blends

Use the words in the box.
Write the missing words to complete the story.

spread	stretches	splash	scream	spring	street

1. It is _____ .

Birds _____

in the puddle.

2. A cat comes by.

The birds _____

bird calls and _____

water on him.

3. The cat runs down the _____ .

4. The cat stops and _____ .

The birds _____ their wings and fly away.

Phonics Practice

Name _____

Initial Three-Letter Blends

Write the word that makes sense in each sentence.

splash   split   street

----

1. At the farm, Jim _____ the firewood.

2. The pig loved to have its

scratched   string   screamed

----

back _____.

splash   split   stripe

----

3. I watched the fish _____ in the pond.

strap   strong   straw

----

4. We gave the barn animals some new _____ .

© Scott, Foresman and Company   G2

For the Birds

Final Consonant Digraphs

Use the letters in the box. Write the letters that end each word.

| ch | sh | th |

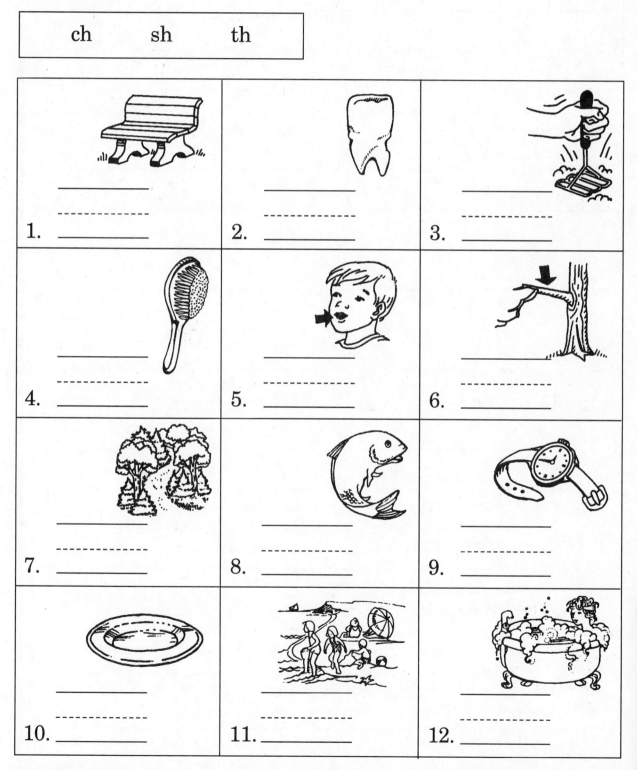

1. _____

2. _____

3. _____

4. _____

5. _____

6. _____

7. _____

8. _____

9. _____

10. _____

11. _____

12. _____

Phonics Review

Name

My Ideas

Name _____

Theme Log

Literature	What I Learned About the Theme	How I Liked the Literature
Molly the Brave and Me		Recommended / Not Recommended
The Relatives Came		Recommended / Not Recommended
Helping Out		Recommended / Not Recommended
Amelia Bedelia Helps Out		Recommended / Not Recommended
The Mother's Day Sandwich		Recommended / Not Recommended
Come Quick!: A Play for April Fool's Day		Recommended / Not Recommended
Hello, Amigos!		Recommended / Not Recommended
Additional Reading		Recommended / Not Recommended
		Recommended / Not Recommended
		Recommended / Not Recommended

Rating Scale Would you recommend the selection to a friend?

Final Consonant Digraphs

Use the letters in the box.
Write the missing letters in the words.

| ch | sh | ng | th |

_____
1. "My too_____ hurts," said Frog.

_____
"I wi_____ I could help," said Toad.

_____   _____
2. "Tea_____ me a so_____,"
said Frog.   _____

They both sa_____ .

_____
3. "Get me a pea_____," said Frog.

_____
They bo_____ ate.

_____
4. Frog's too_____ fell out.

_____
"I feel mu_____ better now,"
said Frog.

Phonics Practice

Realistic Fiction

Complete after reading *Molly the Brave and Me* and *The Relatives Came.*

In realistic fiction characters act like real people. What feelings do Beth and Molly have that real people have?

_____

_____

_____

_____

The things that happen in realistic fiction can happen in real life. List things from each story that could really happen. Use the back of your paper to add more ideas.

Molly the Brave and Me:

_____

_____

The Relatives Came:

_____

_____

Try one of these ideas:

• Realistic fiction is about real people. Think of a real person who could become a character in a story you write. Map some words that describe that person and then use your map to describe this person to a friend.

• Draw a picture of a real place that could be a setting for a story. Save it for later as a realistic fiction story starter.

Molly the Brave and Me

Genre Study

© Scott, Foresman and Company   G2

Vocabulary

Follow the directions for making sentences using the words from *Molly the Brave and Me*. Remember to use your glossary for words you are not sure about.

1. Use the words *country* and *homesick* in a sentence about a trip.

_____

_____

_____

_____

2. Use the words *beetles* and *swatted* in a sentence about a picnic.

_____

_____

_____

_____

3. Use the words *brave, pretended,* and *blinking* in a sentence about the first day at a new school.

_____

_____

_____

_____

Independent Reading Guide

Before You Read

❏ **Preview and Predict:** Read the title and look at the pictures. Which character do you think might be Molly?

As You Read

❏ **Pages 6 to 11:** Find out why Beth wants to be more like Molly.

❏ **Pages 12 to 17:** Read to find out what kinds of things scare Beth. Do you think Molly would be her friend if she found out Beth was afraid sometimes?

TIP! Notice how the author writes about what Beth is thinking so you can tell how she feels.

❏ **Pages 18 to 28:** Find out who is the brave one when Molly and Beth have their adventure.

After You Read

❏ Write down what Molly might have thought when she was lost in the cornfield.

_____

_____

_____

_____

_____

_____

_____

_____

G2

Molly the Brave and Me

Comprehension Check

1. Do you think Molly ever thought Beth was a "wimp"? Tell why you think that way.

_____
_____
_____
_____
_____

2. Tell one way you think Molly and Beth are alike.

_____
_____
_____
_____
_____

3. When Beth got back home, what do you think she told her mom about her weekend?

_____
_____
_____
_____
_____

Draw Conclusions

Fill in the chart with details from
Molly the Brave and Me.

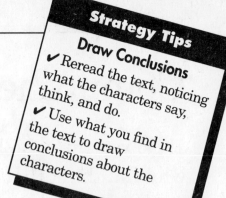

Strategy Tips
Draw Conclusions
✔ Reread the text, noticing what the characters say, think, and do.
✔ Use what you find in the text to draw conclusions about the characters.

Molly

Brave	Not Brave

Conclusion:

_____

- -

_____

- -

_____

Molly the Brave and Me

G2

Vowel Digraphs for Long a (ai, ay)

Use the words in the box. Label the picture.

| nail chain hay pail bluejay mailbox snail |

Phonics Practice

Vowel Digraphs for Long a (ai, ay)

Circle two words in each sentence that have the same vowel sound as *pail* and *say*.

1. Each day I walk out to get the mail.

2. Today there may be something for me.

3. The person who brings the mail is afraid of our dog.

4. We will paint the fence gray.

5. Pete knows the way to the train stop.

6. Jack and Wendy will stay and play with me.

Molly the Brave and Me

Initial Blends

Use the letters in the box. Write the letters that begin the pictured words.

br	cr	fr	gr	tr

1. _____

2. _____

3. _____

4. _____

5. _____

6. _____

7. _____

8. _____

9. _____

10. _____

11. _____

12. _____

Phonics Review

Using Prior Knowledge

Strategy Tips

Use Prior Knowledge
✔ What does the story remind you of?
✔ Use your senses to imagine the story.
✔ Look at the pictures. What is happening in them?

Choose a scene from *The Relatives Came*.
Think of any images, scents, tastes, feelings,
and sounds it makes you think of. Record those things
in the proper box.

What I Would See	What I Would Smell	What I Would Taste	What I Would Hear	What I Would Feel

The Relatives Came

Plural Noun Forms -s and -es

Add *-s* or *-es* to the words below.

1. When Nan and Sue visit their relative_____ ,

they wear their best dress_____ .

2. Grandpa puts out the fancy dish_____
and everyone sits down to eat.

3. They start with soup and cracker_____ .

4. Then they have turkey sandwich_____ .

© Scott, Foresman and Company   G2

The Relatives Came

Phonics Practice

Plural Noun Forms -s and -es

Add -s or -es to the words below. Write the new words.

1. fox _____

2. track _____

3. secret _____

4. glass _____

5. bush _____

6. shirt _____

Write a word from above that makes sense in each sentence.

7. Marco saw a rabbit under

some _____ .

8. The rabbit left _____
in the snow.

The Relatives Came

Medial Digraphs

Read the first word. Circle the other word in the row with the same middle consonant sound.

1. other | together | backyard | homework

2. branches | garden | catchers | bedroom

3. kitchens | people | birdbath | peaches

4. father | across | sunfish | mother

5. watches | munches | wishes | someday

6. breathing | washing | clothing | doghouse

7. feather | crackers | shining | weather

8. marching | lunches | skating | winter

9. another | different | rather | sunset

Phonics Review

Using a Map

1. Write a title for this map.

_____

- -

_____

MAP KEY

★ State capital

● Cities

● Towns

OHIO

PENNSYLVANIA

NEW JERSEY

Wheeling

MARYLAND

WEST VIRGINIA

WASHINGTON, D.C.

DELAWARE

★ Charleston

VIRGINIA

Cool Ridge

KENTUCKY

Richmond ★

Norfolk

Chesapeake

TENNESSEE

NORTH CAROLINA

2. What is the capital of Virginia?

_____

- -

_____

3. Is Cool Ridge a city or a town?

_____

- -

_____

Study Skills

The Relatives Came

© Scott, Foresman and Company   G2

Vocabulary

The following questions include words that you will find in *Helping Out*. You may need to use your glossary to answer these questions.

1. What kinds of things would you see in a *workshop?*

---

2. What *chores* do you like to do?

---

3. What kind of *engine* might need *oil?*

---

4. Ask a question using each of these words. Use your glossary for help.

barnacles

---

scrape

Independent Reading Guide

Before You Read

❑ **Preview and Predict:** The title and pictures give clues about the story. What is this story about?

_____

As You Read

❑ **Pages 54 to 64:** Find out about children helping others. Fill in each job as you read about it. What do you learn about each job? What do you think about each one? Put *yes* or *no* in each box.

Job	Fun	Messy	Hard Work	Easy Work	Inside	Outside

After You Read

❑ Tell about your favorite "helping out" job.

_____

My favorite job is _____ . I like it

_____

because _____ .

Comprehension Check

1. Why do you think George Ancona wrote and photographed *Helping Out?*

_____

_____

_____

_____

2. Do the photographs make *Helping Out* more interesting? Tell why or why not.

_____

_____

_____

3. Describe another picture that could have been included in *Helping Out.*

_____

_____

_____

Name _____

Draw Conclusions

Fill in the diagram showing a job in *Helping Out* and why you would like to do it.

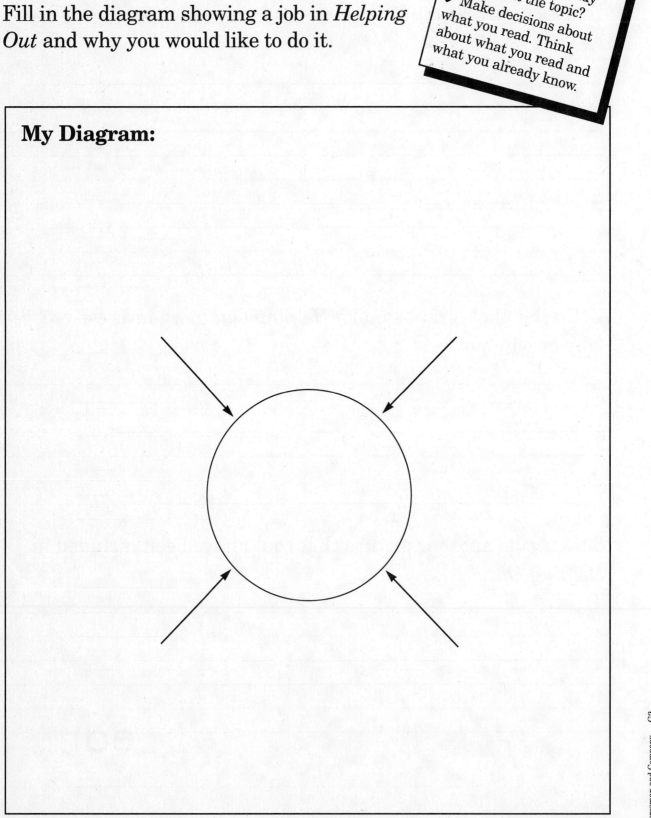

My Diagram:

Helping Out

Vowel Digraphs for Long e (ee, ea)

Write one or two letters on each line to make a word.
Read your words to a friend.

1. _____ eat

2. bea _____

3. _____ eef

4. _____ ree

5. gree _____

6. _____ eet

7. _____ ean

8. fee _____

9. lea _____

10. pea _____

11. tea _____

12. _____ eam

Phonics Practice

Vowel Digraphs for Long e (ee, ea)

Circle three words in each set of sentences that have the same vowel sound as *real* and *wheel*.

Beth planted three seeds in her garden.
Then Beth gave them the water that
they needed.

All the plants soon grew leaves that
reached high. Beth had never seen
plants grow that high.

Next, the plants grew beans. Beth picked
them to feed her brother. Beth and her
brother wanted to eat them for lunch.

Write the words you circled on the lines below.

1. _____   2. _____   3. _____

4. _____   5. _____   6. _____

7. _____   8. _____   9. _____

Helping Out

Initial Blends

Write the word that makes sense in each sentence.

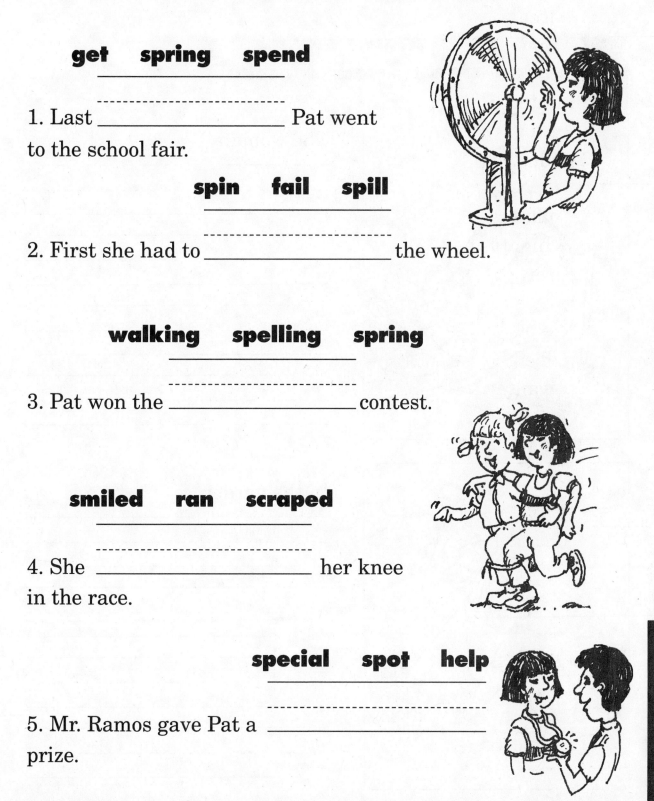

get   spring   spend
_____

1. Last _____ Pat went
to the school fair.

spin   fail   spill
_____

2. First she had to _____ the wheel.

walking   spelling   spring
_____

3. Pat won the _____ contest.

smiled   ran   scraped
_____

4. She _____ her knee
in the race.

special   spot   help
_____

5. Mr. Ramos gave Pat a _____
prize.

Phonics Review

Vocabulary

Use any of the words below to finish the sentences.

**dust fret quilt scraps sew
sow stake steak weed teacake**

The woman

_____

- -

_____

- -

_____

- -

_____

- -

_____

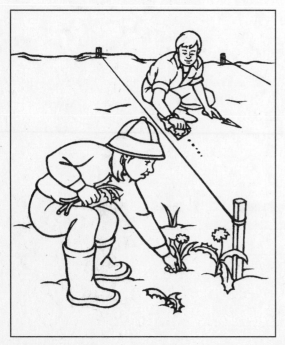

In the garden,

_____

- -

_____

- -

_____

- -

_____

- -

_____

Amelia Bedelia Helps Out

Independent Reading Guide

Before You Read

❏ **Preview and Predict:** Amelia Bedelia is a character who often makes a mess of things. What do you think will happen when Amelia tries to help out?

As You Read

❏ **Pages 66 to 79:** Amelia Bedelia is given some work to do. As you read, take notes on what she actually does!

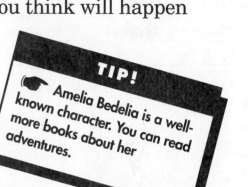

TIP!
Amelia Bedelia is a well-known character. You can read more books about her adventures.

Miss Emma's Orders	What Amelia Bedelia Does
1. Weed the garden.	1.
2. Stake the beans.	2.
3. Dust the bugs.	3.
4. Give scraps to the chickens.	4.
5. Bake a tea cake.	5.
6. Sow grass seeds on the lawn.	6.

❏ **Pages 80 to 88:** Find out what happens at the party. How do you think Miss Emma feels about Amelia Bedelia's help?

After You Read

❏ Suppose you told Amelia Bedelia to "put out" the lights after she finished her work. What do you think she would do?

Comprehension Check

1. Is there anything that Amelia Bedelia does *right?* Explain.

_____

- -

_____

- -

_____

- -

_____

2. What kind of scraps does Miss Emma want Amelia Bedelia to give the chickens?

_____

- -

_____

- -

_____

- -

_____

3. If you were Miss Emma, would you ask Amelia Bedelia to come back and help again? Tell why or why not.

_____

- -

_____

- -

_____

- -

_____

Amelia Bedelia Helps Out

Read On

Find a sentence in *Amelia Bedelia Helps Out* that is hard to understand. Tell what you could do to figure it out.

Text	Comments

Vowel Digraphs for Long i (ie, igh)

Write the missing words to complete the poem.

Light Pie Delight

tried   tread
_____
- -

Although she _____

might   mart
_____
- - - - - - - - - - - - - - - - - - - -

with all her _____ ,

Miss Knight could never

rot   right
_____
- - - - - - - - - - - - - - - - - - - -

get things _____ .

She thought her

pie   put
_____
- - - - - - - - - - - - - - - - - - -

light mint _____ delight

Could not be served

lost   light
_____
- - - - - - - - - - - - - - - - - - -

without a _____ .

Phonics Practice

Amelia Bedelia Helps Out

Vowel Digraphs for Long i (ie, igh)

Circle two words in each set of sentences that have the same vowel sound you hear in *pie* and *tight*.

1. It was a dark, stormy night.
The howling wind frightened Joe.

2. "Lie down and go to sleep," said Mom.
"Turn out the light."

3. Joe tried to get to sleep.
"It's no use," he sighed.

4. Then lightning flashed.
"Oh, no!" he cried.

5. The bright flash lit up his room.
He pried the window open.

6. It was a beautiful sight.
He might even learn not to be afraid of storms.

Extra Phonics Practice

Plural Nouns - s

Circle the word that goes with each picture.

1. sun

   suns

2. boys

   boy

3. house

   houses

4. door

   doors

5. plants

   plant

6. hat

   hats

7. truck

   trucks

8. bikes

   bike

9. dolls

   doll

10. ball

    balls

11. girl

    girls

12. birds

    bird

Amelia Bedelia Helps Out

Phonics Review

Vocabulary

These words can describe a kitchen. Use each word in a
sentence about a kitchen. Use your glossary if you need help.

cabinet

counter

container

allowed

tiptoed

toppled

arranged

Independent Reading Guide

Before You Read

❑ **Preview and Predict:** What special day do you think this story is about?

As You Read

❑ **Pages 90 to 101:** Read to find out how Ivy and Hackett decide to surprise their mother.

❑ **Pages 102 to 104:** What does a Mother's Day sandwich look like? Read to find out. Draw a picture of a Mother's Day sandwich when you find out what it is.

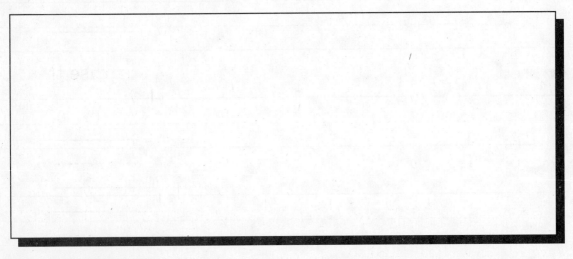

After You Read

❑ How do you think Mama felt when she found the mess the children made in the kitchen? What would you do if you were Mama?

The Mother's Day Sandwich

Comprehension Check

1. Draw a picture of how the kitchen looks after Ivy and Hackett finish making Mama's breakfast.

2. Why do you think Ivy and Hackett want to surprise their mother on Mother's Day?

3. Do you think Ivy and Hackett get along well together? Tell why you think that way.

Using Context

Write how you would figure out the
unfamiliar word. Read these sentences
from *The Mother's Day Sandwich*.

Strategy Tips

Understanding Words

✔ Can you skip the word?
✔ Look for clues to
meaning.
✔ Look at the letters of
the word. Do you know
any words that begin or
end in the same way?
✔ Make sure your guess
makes sense.

Text	How to Figure It Out
"Hackett opened the **refrigerator**." (p. 92)	
"At last everything was neatly **arranged** on the tray." (p. 98)	
"The tray **toppled** over." (p. 101)	
"Well, you **certainly** surprised me," she said, laughing." (p. 102)	

Name _____

Vowel Digraphs for Long o (oa, oe, ow)

Use the words in the box.
Write the missing words to complete the story.

bowls	yellow	tiptoed	groaned	toast	soaked

1. We _____ into Dad's

room with _____ of soup,

roast beef on _____,

_____ apples,

root beer floats.

2. We woke up Dad.
Everything spilled and

_____ the bed.

3. Dad just _____

and shook his head.

The Mother's Day Sandwich

Practice Book 125

© Scott, Foresman and Company G2

Phonics Practice

Vowel Digraphs for Long o
(oa, oe, ow)

Circle two words in each set of sentences that have the same
vowel sound you hear in *boat*, *goes*, and *row*.

1. It snowed last night.
I put on my socks to keep my toes warm.

2. I put on my coat and boots.
Then I put on my yellow hat and went out.

3. My sister followed me.
We ran to the oak tree.

4. Then we made a snowman.
We used coal for his eyes.

5. "Let's show Mom," said my sister.
"I know she'll like it."

6. After playing, we were wet and snowy.
We went inside to have some hot cocoa.

The Mother's Day Sandwich

© Scott, Foresman and Company   G2

Vowel Digraphs ai and ay

Circle the words that have the same vowel sound as
pail and *say*.

1. Ella and Zip were frogs.
Zip was afraid of water.

2. One gray morning, Ella had an idea.
Maybe she could help Zip play
in the water.

3. They hopped down the trail to
the pond. Zip carried the pail.

4. On the way they met Sam Snail.
"May I come along?" he asked.

5. It started to rain. Zip, Sam,
and Ella played tag in the pond.

6. Now Zip stays in the water
every day!

Phonics Review

Vocabulary

Draw a picture to explain the meaning of each word. Use your glossary if you are unsure about a word's meaning.

gorilla

seal

snake

wriggling

Come Quick!

Independent Reading Guide

Before You Read

❏ **Preview and Predict:** What is the play about? How many people are in the play? Look at the things you will need. What will you do with these things? What do you think might happen during the play?

TIP!

The words in slanted type show you what a character is doing while saying the speaking parts of a play.

As You Read

❏ **Pages 110 to 114:** Read the play to find out who really gets fooled on April Fool's Day!

After You Read

❏ Find a partner, make the props, and read the play together. Be sure to do the actions for each character.

Come Quick!

Comprehension Check

1. How do you think the father feels when the boy keeps running back into the living room? Explain.

_____

- -

_____

- -

_____

2. Why is the boy surprised when his father says there are animals in the boy's bedroom?

_____

- -

_____

- -

_____

3. Do you think the boy played a good April Fool's Day trick? Tell why or why not.

_____

- -

_____

- -

_____

Skim and Scan

Flip through the pages of a book. Write things that help you think about what you will read. Draw a poster with the hints on it.

What helps you plan reading?

1. _____

2. _____

3. _____

Sketch your poster here:

Contractions

Find and underline five contractions in this letter.
Write the two words that make up each contraction
on the lines below.

July 7

Dear Mom,

   I'm having lots of fun at camp. Don't
forget to feed my fish.

   I've made a new friend. She'd like to
visit us later this summer. We'll see you
soon!

Love, Suzy

---

1. _____   _____

2. _____   _____

3. _____   _____

4. _____   _____

5. _____   _____

G2

Phonics Practice

Come Quick!

Contractions

Read each sentence and look at the underlined word. Circle the two words that make up the contraction.

---

1. <u>He's</u> not able to finish his work.

   He will   Where is   He is

---

2. I <u>couldn't</u> drink the water.

   could not   can not   was not

---

3. <u>We'll</u> go to my friend's house after school.

   We have   Where will   We will

---

4. <u>I've</u> been there before.

   They have   I have   I will

---

5. Monday <u>we're</u> returning home.

   they are   we are   we have

---

6. <u>They've</u> been to the basketball game.

   I have   They will   They have

Extra Phonics Practice

Vowel Digraphs ee and ea

Circle the words in each sentence that have the same vowel sound as *leaf* and *bee*.

1. Kevin planted some seeds in his yard. He wanted to grow green beans.

2. Kevin would peek at them in the morning. Each day he would water and feed his plants.

3. In a week the plants started to grow. Kevin pulled weeds to clear his garden.

4. The plants grew and grew. Soon Kevin couldn't reach the top. He had never seen such tall plants!

5. Kevin cleaned the beans for a big feast. His friends came by to eat.

Vocabulary

Follow the directions for making sentences using the words from *Hello, Amigos!* Remember to use your glossary for words you are not sure about.

1. Use the words *amigos* and *blessings* in a sentence about being thankful.

_____

_____

_____

2. Use the words *avocados* and *guacamole* in a sentence about a snack.

_____

_____

_____

3. Use the words *lesson, recess,* and *sling* in a sentence about school.

_____

_____

_____

Independent Reading Guide

Before You Read

❏ **Preview and Predict:** What do the pictures tell you about Frankie Valdez? Does he do any of the things you do each day? Does something special happen?

As You Read

❏ **Pages 117 to 123:** Read to find out about Frankie Valdez. Why is Frankie so happy and excited? What's the best thing that happened?

Frankie's Day	
morning	
afternoon	
nighttime	

❏ **Pages 124 to 132:** Find out how Frankie and his family celebrate his birthday.

After You Read

❏ Pretend today's your birthday. List two special things you would like to have happen.

_____

- -

_____

- -

_____

G2

Hello Amigos!

Comprehension Check

1. Do you think Frankie likes going to school on his birthday? Explain why you think that way.

_____
_____
_____
_____

2. If you were Frankie, what would be your favorite part of your birthday? Tell why.

_____
_____
_____
_____

3. Is Frankie's birthday like your birthday? Tell how your birthday is like Frankie's, or how it is different.

_____
_____
_____
_____
_____

Compare and Contrast

Compare other things Frankie does in *Hello Amigos!* to what you and your friends do.

Frankie			

Variable Digraph ea

Can you answer these riddles about food?
Use the words in the box and write the answers.

tea	peanuts	meats	peach	bread	breakfast

1. What does every sandwich have?

   _____

   -

   _____

2. What drink do people like either hot or with ice?

   _____

   -

   _____

3. Turkey, beef, and chicken are called _____.

   _____

   -

   _____

4. What fruit is yellow and orange and fuzzy?

   _____

   -

   _____

5. Every morning I have a big _____.

   _____

   -

   _____

6. Something elephants like to eat:

   _____

   -

   _____

G2

Phonics Practice

Variable Sounds for the Digraph ea

Use the words in the box.
Write a word to answer each riddle.

| heat | thread | beat | bread | peach | head |

---

1. I am a noise made by a drum.
   What am I?

   _____
   - - - - - - - - - - - - -

2. I am something to eat.
   I am part of a sandwich.
   What am I?

   _____
   - - - - - - - - - - - - -

3. I am part of your body.
   I sit on your neck.
   What am I?

   _____
   - - - - - - - - - - - - -

4. I come from a fire or a furnace. You need me when it is cold outside. What am I?

   _____
   - - - - - - - - - - - - -

5. You can use me when you sew. You push me through a needle. What am I?

   _____
   - - - - - - - - - - - - -

6. My skin is soft and fuzzy.
   I am a kind of fruit.
   What am I?

   _____
   - - - - - - - - - - - - -

Hello Amigo!

Vowel Digraphs ow

Say the first word in the row.
Circle the word that has the same
vowel sound.

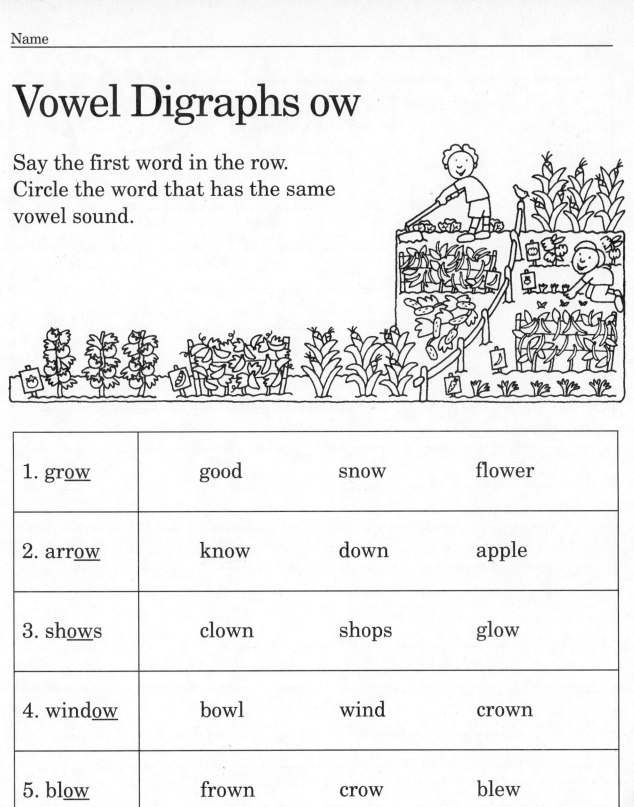

1. gr<u>ow</u>	good	snow	flower
2. arr<u>ow</u>	know	down	apple
3. sh<u>ow</u>s	clown	shops	glow
4. wind<u>ow</u>	bowl	wind	crown
5. bl<u>ow</u>	frown	crow	blew
6. pill<u>ow</u>	gown	pound	tow

Phonics Review

My Ideas

Theme Log

Literature	What I Learned About the Theme	How I Liked the Literature
A Pet for the Goofs		
Do-It-Yourself Experiments		
Tomás and the Library Lady		
My Dog and the Green Sock Mystery		
The Tortoise and the Hare		
The Monkey and the Pea/The Big Fish Who Wasn't So Big		
Animal Babies		
Buffy's Orange Leash		
Additional Reading		

Rating Scale ★★★★ great ★★★ good ★★ average ★ poor

How many stars?

Vocabulary

The following questions include words that you will find in *A Pet for the Goofs*. You may need to use your glossary to answer these questions.

1. What does a *librarian* do?

_____

- -

_____

2. What is one kind of animal that wears a *collar?*

_____

- -

_____

3. What is something that can make a person feel *terrible?*

_____

- -

_____

4. Ask a question using each of these words. Use your glossary for help.

goofy

_____

- -

wonderful

_____

- -

Independent Reading Guide

Before You Read

❑ **Preview and Predict:** What does the title tell you about the story? Do you think the story is about real people?

TIP! Look up the word goofy before you read the story.

As You Read

❑ **Pages 6 to 8:** As you read, look at the pictures closely. The pictures give clues about the family. How would you describe the Goofs?

❑ **Pages 9 to 11:** Find out what kind of pet the Goofs THINK they found. Why do they think their pet is sad?

❑ **Pages 12 to 13:** Read to find out if the Goofs ever figure out what their pet really is.

❑ **Pages 14 to 16:** How did the authors invent the Goofs?

After You Read

❑ Draw a picture of the Goofs on a picnic that shows how "goofy" they are!

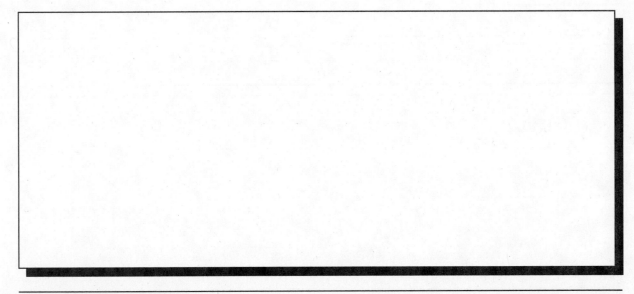

Comprehension Check

1. If you were the turtle, would you like living with the Goofs?
Tell why or why not.

_____

_____

_____

_____

2. Do you think the Goofs will ever find out what their pet
really is? Tell why you think that way.

_____

_____

_____

_____

3. Do you think the Goofs know they are goofy? Explain.

_____

_____

_____

_____

A Pet for the Goofs

© Scott, Foresman and Company   G2

Details and Facts

Write what Big Goof and Little Goof say
and do. Write how they look in the pictures.
What are they like?

Strategy Tips

Analyzing Characters

✔ Read carefully. What do characters say and do?

✔ Look at the pictures. How do characters look and act?

✔ Add up the details. What are the characters like?

What I Read	**What I See**

What I Think About Big Goof and Little Goof

Verb Endings Without Spelling Changes -s, -es, -ed, -ing

Add *-s, -es, -ing,* or *-ed* to the words in the story.

Big Goof kept reading.
_____

1. "A dog eat_____ dog food."
_____

"But Doggie just mess_____ it up!"
said Little Goof.
_____

2. "A dog like_____ to fetch a stick,"
read Big Goof.
_____

"But Doggie just look_____ at it,"
said Little Goof.
_____

3. "A dog's fur need_____ to be
_____

brush_____ ," read Big Goof.
"But Doggie has lost all his fur!"
said Little Goof.
_____

4. "Doggie look_____ mad.
_____

He's walk_____ away," said Little Goof.

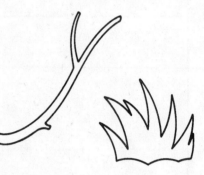

© Scott, Foresman and Company G2

A Pet for the Goofs

Verb Endings Without Spelling Changes -s, -es, -ed, -ing

Underline the word that makes sense in each sentence.

1. Pat ____ to write a report about magnets.

    needs   needing

2. She went to the library and began ____ for a book.

    looking   looked

3. She saw that a book was ____.

    falls   falling

4. Pat ____ it up. It was about magnets!

    picked   picking

Write each word without its ending.

5. falling

_____

- - - - - - - - - - - - - - -

_____

6. needs

_____

- - - - - - - - - - - - - - -

_____

7. picked

_____

- - - - - - - - - - - - - - -

_____

8. looking

_____

- - - - - - - - - - - - - - -

_____

Extra Phonics Practice

Vowel Digraphs ie, igh

Underline two words in each sentence that have the same vowel sound you hear in *tie* and *fight*.

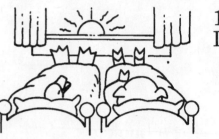

1. The bright light woke up Pig and Duck.

2. Pig cried, "The sun is a beautiful sight!"

3. Pig pried his sand bucket out of the tightly packed toybox.

4. Pig tries to stay clean when he plays, but he is usually dirty each night.

5. You might say that Duck stays cleaner when he plays and you would be right!

G2

A Pet for the Goofs

Making a Chart

1. Write a title for the chart.

_____

- -

_____

2. Complete the chart.

Features	Birds	Dogs
Number of feet	2	4
Number of eyes		
Have wings		
Number of ears	2	
Have feathers	Yes	No
Have fur		
Have a tail		
Have teeth	No	
Can swim		
Can walk		
Sound it makes	Tweets	Barks

Study Skills

Vocabulary

These words are from *Do-It-Yourself Experiments*. How much do you know about these words? Put an X below your answer.

Word	I know what this word means.	I have seen or heard this word.	I don't know what this word means.
static electricity			
faucet			
fingerprints			
comparing			
smudged			
forearm			
measuring tape			

Now use two of the vocabulary words you know in a sentence. Remember to check your glossary for words you are unsure about.

G2

Do-It-Yourself Experiments

Independent Reading Guide

Before You Read

❑ **Preview and Predict:** What is different about the print in *Do-It-Yourself Experiments?* Will there be characters? Will there be a story?

As You Read

❑ **Pages 18 to 26:** Read the directions. Do the experiments. Record your results.

TIP!
☞ If you don't have equipment, just do the activities that do not require materials.

Body Tricks	**Balancing Act**	**Quick!**
Can you hop backward?	What number did you count to?	Which is bigger, your foot or your forearm?

Fingerprints	**Lost and Found**	**Elec-tricks**
Which type is most common? Which type do you have?	Is the coin still there? What happens to the pencil?	What happens to: the balloon? the paper? the water?

After You Read

❑ Which experiment had a result that surprised you?

What did you expect to happen?

Comprehension Check

1. Which experiment interests you the most? Tell why.

_____

- -

_____

- -

_____

- -

_____

- -

_____

2. Do the pictures help you understand how to do the experiments? Explain why or why not.

_____

- -

_____

- -

_____

- -

_____

3. What makes water wiggle? Tell what you know.

_____

- -

_____

- -

_____

- -

_____

© Scott, Foresman and Company   G2

Do-It-Yourself Experiments

Name

Following Directions

Fill in the chart below with information from the second "Elek-Trick" on p. 24 of *Do-It-Yourself Experiments.*

Strategy Tips

Following Directions

- ✔ Read words in dark type. They tell what the experiment is about.
- ✔ Look for details about the materials you need.
- ✔ Follow the numbered steps.

What I Want to Know
What Materials I Need
What I Do
What I Learned

Verb Endings with Spelling Changes -ed, -ing

Write the root word for each underlined verb.

_____

1. Scott <u>rubbed</u> a balloon on his hair. _____

2. He <u>grinned</u>. _____

3. "I'm <u>coming</u> to get you," he said to Sue. _____

4. Sue <u>stared</u> at him. _____

5. She <u>patted</u> his head. _____

6. Then she <u>popped</u> the balloon and Scott jumped. _____

7. "I <u>scared</u> you instead!" she said. _____

Do-It-Yourself Experiments

Phonics Practice

G2

Verb Endings with Spelling Changes -ed, -ing

Underline the word that makes sense in each sentence.

1. Jamie was sick in bed.

Sara ____ pictures
in a book for him.

pasting   pasted

2. She brought the book with
more pictures and some glue.

Jamie liked ____ pictures
in the book.

gluing   glued

3. Sara ____ from ear to ear.

grinning   grinned

Write each word without an ending.

pasted   **gluing**   **grinned**

_____   _____   _____

- - - - - - - - - - -   - - - - - - - - - - -   - - - - - - - - - - -

_____   _____   _____

Extra Phonics Practice

Initial Blends

Use the letters in the box. Write the letters that begin each pictured word.

| sc | sm | st | str |

1. _____

2. _____

3. _____

4. _____

5. _____

6. _____

7. _____

8. _____

9. _____

10. _____

11. _____

12. _____

Do-It-Yourself Experiments

Phonics Review

© Scott, Foresman and Company   G2

Prior Knowledge

Fill in each column of the chart.

Strategy Tips
Prior Knowledge
✔ What do characters do? How do they feel?
✔ Have you ever acted or felt the same way?
✔ Use what you know to understand characters.

Story Details	Using Prior Knowledge	How I Think Tomás Feels

Syllable Division

Find and underline the eight two-syllable words in the story. Write the words on the lines below. Draw a line between the two syllables.

One day, a little yellow cat followed
Sammy home. His mom said he could keep
it if he could take care of it.

He read books that told how to care for
kittens and cats. He borrowed books all summer.
Now he and his cat are happy.

Tomás and the Library Lady

Syllable Division

Put the syllables together to make a word. Write the word.

pup pet _____ hur ry _____

fun ny _____ mit ten _____

Write a word from the box that makes sense in each sentence.

1. This may look like just a _____ , but it's much more than that.

2. When Mom adds a few things to it,

it turns into my _____ , Slinky!

3. When it snows, Slinky becomes a

mitten again in a _____ !

Extra Phonics Practice

Verb Endings -s and -ed

Add the s and ed endings to these words.

s	ed

1. bump _____ _____

2. peek _____ _____

3. roar _____ _____

4. pick _____ _____

5. curl _____ _____

6. jump _____ _____

7. howl _____ _____

8. work _____ _____

© Scott, Foresman and Company   G2

Tomás and the Library Lady

Phonics Review

Vocabulary

The following questions include words that you will find in *My Dog and the Green Sock Mystery*. You may need to use your glossary to answer these questions.

1. How does a *sloppy* room look?

_____

_____

2. Who often *solves* mysteries or problems in your family?

_____

_____

3. What kinds of things have *disappeared* at home or at school?

_____

_____

4. What do people usually do if their clothes have *wrinkles* in them?

_____

_____

Independent Reading Guide

Before You Read

❏ **Preview and Predict:** Read the title of the story. What is the mystery? What character is connected to the mystery?

As You Read

❏ **Pages 44 to 47:** As you read, be a detective yourself and make a list of Andy's missing things.

❏ **Pages 48 to 53:** Read to find out what important clues Jennie learns about Andy.

❏ **Pages 54 to 60:** Jennie believes My Dog is a real detective. Andy disagrees. Do you think My Dog will find the missing things? Read on to find out.

After You Read

❏ My Dog is lost again! Help her find her way home.

My Dog and the Green Sock Mystery

Comprehension Check

1. Who solves the mystery in this story? Tell why you think that way.

_____

----

2. Do Jennie and Andy feel the same way about My Dog? Explain.

_____

----

3. Would you want My Dog to be *your* dog? Explain why or why not.

_____

Predict Outcomes

Choose another mystery to read. Fill in the chart below to predict what will happen in the story.

What I Read +	What I Know =	What I Predict

My Dog and the Green Sock Mystery

G2

Prefixes pre-, dis-

Use the prefixes *pre-* or *dis-*.
Write the prefix that makes sense in each word.

1. My friends and I played a baseball game. We sang "Take

Me Out to the Ball Game" for our _____ game show.

2. My little sister brought friends from her _____school.

3. My mom brought our dog, Gus, to the game and told him to sit.

Gus _____obeyed and ran onto the field.

4. When everybody laughed, he thought people _____liked him.

5. He _____appeared under the seats.

Prefixes pre-, dis-

Add a word from the box to each prefix to make new
words that make sense in the sentences.

| agreed | views | school | liked | heat | connect |

1. When my little sister came home from

_____

pre_____, Mom let us watch a movie on
videotape.

2. I thought the pre_____ were better than
the movie.

3. My sister dis_____ .

4. I dis_____ the ending of the movie.

5. I wanted to dis_____ the TV set!
Instead, I went to the kitchen.

6. I helped Mom pre_____ a pan to pop popcorn.

My Dog and the Green Sock Mystery

Contractions

Write the contraction for each pair of words.

1. can not _____

2. I am _____

3. should not _____

4. I will _____

5. does not _____

6. did not _____

7. was not _____

8. she is _____

9. is not _____

10. they will _____

11. we will _____

12. he is _____

13. you will _____

14. could not _____

Phonics Review

Fable

Complete after reading *The Monkey and the Pea* and *The Big Fish Who Wasn't So Big*.

Animals in fables often act like people. List at least three ways the tortoise and the hare act like people.

_____

- -

_____

- -

_____

- -

_____

- -

Fables often have a moral or lesson. Tell lessons from *The Monkey and the Pea* or *The Big Fish Who Wasn't So Big* in your own words.

_____

- -

_____

- -

_____

- -

_____

- -

Try one of these ideas:
- Fables have lessons we can learn. Think of a lesson that you might want to use a fable to tell. Tell a friend how you might write a story about the lesson.
- Draw a picture of an animal you might write about in a fable. Show the animal both before and after learning a lesson.

Genre Study

The Tortoise and the Hare

© Scott, Foresman and Company   G2

Vocabulary

These words can describe a race. Use each word in a sentence about a race. Use your glossary if you need help.

flashy

---

rude

---

slowpoke

---

victory

---

perseverance

---

reward

Write a sentence about a race. Use at least one of the words above in your sentence.

Independent Reading Guide

Before You Read

❏ **Preview and Predict:** Look at the pictures. What do you notice about the characters in the story? Which character do you think you might like better?

As You Read

❏ **Pages 64 to 71:** Why do you think Hare wants to run a race with Tortoise? Find out what Tortoise decides to do.

❏ **Pages 72 to 81:** Who wins the big race? What lesson does Hare learn? What lesson does Tortoise learn?

After You Read

❏ Write your own fable with the moral:

Hard work and perseverance bring reward.

The Tortoise and the Hare

Comprehension Check

1. Why do you think Hare wanted to race against Tortoise?

_____

- -

_____

- -

_____

2. How do you think Hare felt at the end of the race? Tell why
you think that way.

_____

- -

_____

- -

_____

3. Do you think the training that Tortoise did helped him win
the race? Explain why or why not.

_____

- -

_____

- -

Details and Facts

Tortoise and Hare want to have another contest. What kind of contest should they have? What do you know about Tortoise and Hare that will help you predict what will happen?

Type of Contest: _____

What I Know About Tortoise	What I Know About Hare	I Predict . . .

The Tortoise and the Hare

R-Controlled Vowels ar, or

Use the words in the box. Label the picture.

| corn | forks | horse | car | garden | porch | barn |

Phonics Practice

R-Controlled Vowels ar, or

Circle the word in each box that has the same vowel sound as the picture.

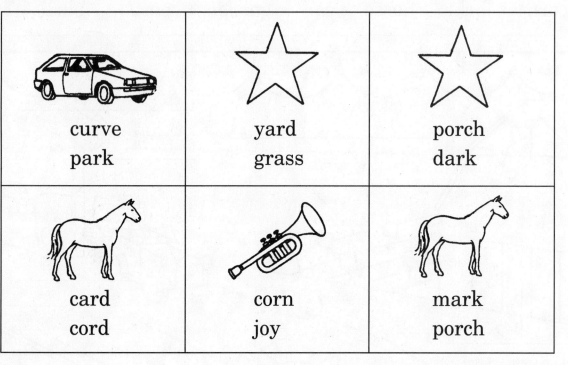

curve park	yard grass	porch dark
card cord	corn joy	mark porch

Use two of the words you circled to complete each sentence.

1. We like to play at

_____

----

the _____ .

2. "Oh, no," said the farmer.
"A cow is eating the

_____

_____ !"

The Tortoise and the Hare

Verb Endings -ed and -ing

Read each sentence. Find the root word of the underlined word and circle it.

1. Tortoise kept on <u>stirring</u> the potato soup.

   stirs   **stirred**   **stir**

2. He <u>smiled</u> as he thought about the race.

   smiles   **smile**   **smiling**

3. Everyone was <u>clapping</u> for him.

   claps   **clapped**   **clap**

4. All the animals <u>teased</u> Hare after the race.

   tease   **teasing**   **teases**

5. Why had Hare <u>stopped</u> to rest?

   stops   **stop**   **stopping**

6. Tortoise was <u>closing</u> the door when he saw Hare.

   close   **closes**   **closed**

7. Hare <u>hopped</u> over to talk to Tortoise.

   hops   **hopping**   **hop**

8. Hare and Tortoise smiled and <u>hugged</u>.

   hugged   **hug**   **hugs**

Phonics Review

Vocabulary

Write sentences below using the words from *The Monkey and the Pea* and *The Big Fish Who Wasn't So Big*. Remember to use your glossary for words you are not sure about.

1. Use the words *needlessly* and *upset* in a sentence about spilled milk.

_____

_____

2. Use the words *gobbled, greedy,* and *huge* in a sentence about a meal.

_____

_____

3. Use the words *enormous, important,* and *peaceful* in a sentence about an animal.

_____

_____

4. Use the words *puny* and *unimportant* in a sentence about another animal.

_____

_____

Independent Reading Guide

Before You Read

❏ **Preview and Predict:** Who are the main characters in each story? Predict which character is greedy. Predict which one thinks he is better than everyone else.

As You Read

❏ **Read pages 86 to 89:** Using your own words, tell what the following words mean:

He lost a handful needlessly
By chasing after one small pea.

❏ **Pages 90 to 94:** Read to find out about a fish who thought BIGGER was better. What lesson does the fish learn?

After You Read

❏ Big fish changes his behavior. The greedy little monkey doesn't. Write down what you would tell the monkey so he wouldn't be greedy anymore.

Comprehension Check

The Monkey and the Pea

1. What do you think the monkey will do the next time he finds some peas?

_____

_____

_____

_____

The Big Fish Who Wasn't So Big

2. Did the big fish change in this fable? Explain your answer.

_____

_____

_____

_____

3. Do you think *The Big Fish Who Wasn't So Big* is a good name for this fable? Tell why or why not.

_____

_____

_____

_____

Generalize

Compare and contrast details from *The Big Fish Who Wasn't So Big* and *The Monkey and the Pea* to *The Tortoise and the Hare*. What do the fables have in common?

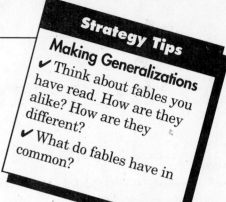

Strategy Tips

Making Generalizations

✔ Think about fables you have read. How are they alike? How are they different?

✔ What do fables have in common?

The Tortoise and the Hare	The Monkey and the Pea	What Both Fables Have in Common

The Tortoise and the Hare	The Big Fish Who Wasn't So Big	What Both Fables Have in Common

Prefixes re-, un-

Use the prefix *re-* or *un-*. Write the prefix that makes sense in each word. Then finish the story on another piece of paper.

1. Monkey was very _____ happy.

2. He thought it was _____ fair that

the prince didn't bring food for him.

Later that day, the prince came back

carrying a box.

3. When he _____ covered the box,

Monkey jumped. The box spilled.

The prince tried to _____ fill it.

4. He was _____ able to stop Monkey,

who took everything. When Monkey

really looked at what he had taken,

he was _____ sure about

whether he wanted it.

© Scott, Foresman and Company   G2

Phonics Practice

The Monkey/The Big Fish

Prefixes re-, un-

Add a word from the box to each prefix to make new words that make sense in the sentences.

| cook paint lock roll happy |

1. It's time to un _____ your sleeping bag.

2. She will re _____ the house.

3. The baby was un _____.

4. I am going to re _____ the chicken.

5. We tried to un _____ the door.

Extra Phonics Practice

Syllable Division

Put the syllables together to make a word. Write the word.

1. mid dle _____   2. sum mer _____

3. gob ble _____   4. hur ry _____

5. sil ly _____   6. sud den _____

7. lit tle _____   8. col lect _____

9. kit ten _____   10. din ner _____

11. par rot _____   12. fol low _____

The Monkey/The Big Fish

© Scott, Foresman and Company   G2

Vocabulary

Use at least one of the words below to finish the sentences.

**discover   exploring   instinct   intelligent   object
perform   romping   squabbles**

The puppy

_____

- -

_____

- -

_____

- -

_____

The kittens

_____

- -

_____

- -

_____

- -

_____

Independent Reading Guide

Before You Read

❏ **Preview and Predict:** Look at the pages of *Animal Babies*. What do the pictures tell you about the story? What is the same in the pictures? Is anything different?

As You Read

❏ **Pages 96 to 100:** How do animal babies know what to eat? How do they learn to live with other animals? Read to find out about things baby animals know and things they must learn. Fill in the chart as you read.

Animal	What the animal knows	What the animal needs to learn

After You Read

❏ Think about how you have changed since you were a baby. Write two things you have learned to do.

Comprehension Check

1. You are a scientist who studies how animals learn. Which animal in this article would you most like to watch? Tell why.

_____

_____

_____

2. What would happen to a puppy if it couldn't play? Explain.

_____

_____

_____

3. What are some things that all baby animals have to learn?

_____

_____

_____

_____

Classify

Read the facts and details from *Animal Babies*. Write information under the correct head. If you want, add other information for each head.

Chick	Foal	Puppy	Bear	Dolphin

has yellow feathers
baby horse
has 4 legs
leaps through hoops
lives in water
plays basketball
has instincts
fights for a stick
romps

pecks at hard, shiny objects
has teeth
has a tail
has a beak
gets food from its mother
learns where to find food

has fur
eats fish
learns by playing
eats salmon and bird eggs
has a tongue
has 2 eyes
has 2 ears
learns what to eat

Animal Babies

R-Controlled Vowels -er, -ir, -ur

Use the words in the box.
Write the words to complete the poem.

Bird	served	hurt	squirmy	blurt	dessert	turns

Bird Alert

1. Squirmy worms squirm

_____

At the thought of getting _____

_____

Or being _____ to baby birds

_____

For dinner or _____ .

_____   _____

2. So _____ worms take _____

Serving duty in the dirt.

A squirmy worm on bird patrol

_____   _____

Must _____ out, " _____ Alert!"

© Scott, Foresman and Company   G2

Phonics Practice

R-Controlled Vowels -er, -ir

Name the picture in each box. Circle the word that has the same vowel sound as the picture.

corn perch	girl car	storm her

Use the words you circled to complete each sentence.

1. At first the _____
was afraid of the bird.

2. Then she saw the bird
_____
_____ on her
friend's finger.

3. She knew then that the bird
_____
wouldn't hurt _____ .

Animal Babies

R-Controlled Vowels ar, or

Name the picture in each box. Circle the word that has the same vowel sound as the picture.

1.	2.	3.
farm store	corn jar	sore move
4.	5.	6.
hole horn	large born	came floor
7.	8.	9.
fork dark	sort start	sport find
10.	11.	12.
farm cork	lord start	leap dark

Phonics Review

Vocabulary

These words are from *Buffy's Orange Leash*. How much do you know about these words? Put an X below your answer.

Word	I know what this word means.	I have seen or heard this word.	I don't know what this word means.
ordinary			
sign language			
smoke detector			
trainers			

Now use two of the vocabulary words you know in a sentence. Remember to check your glossary for words you are unsure about.

_____

_____

_____

_____

_____

_____

_____

_____

Independent Reading Guide

Before You Read

❑ **Preview and Predict:** Who is Buffy? Why do you think Buffy's orange leash is important to the story?

As You Read

❑ **Pages 104 to 109:** Read to find out why Buffy is a special dog.

❑ **Pages 110 to 116:** How does Buffy help the Johnsons? Make a list of things Buffy does for his family.

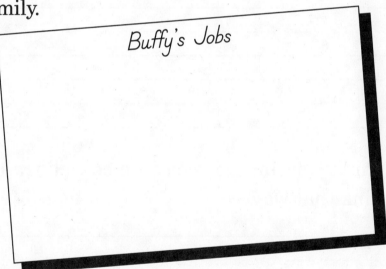

Buffy's Jobs

After You Read

❑ Practice the signs for "Hello, friend." Use the signs next time you meet your friends.

Hello!   **friend**

(like a salute)

Name

Comprehension Check

1. What is one thing you have learned about Hearing Dogs?

2. The trainers picked Buffy because he liked to listen. Why was listening important?

3. Do you think Hearing Dogs have to be well trained? Explain why you think that way.

194 Practice Book

Buffy's Orange Leash

© Scott, Foresman and Company   G2

Predict from Previewing

Look at a book you haven't read before.
Tell what the picture on each page shows.
Predict what you think the story might be about
after looking at each picture. Tell what you want to find out.

Page Number	What the Picture Shows	What I Predict	What I Want to Find Out

Silent Consonants

Use the words in the box.
Write the words to complete the poem.

| right   bought   Though   doubt   know |

Fix It! Quick!

_____

We _____ this last night,

_____

But it doesn't work _____ .

It leaves silent consonants out!

_____

_____ I write with it quickly,

This typewriter's sickly.

_____

You'll _____ how to fix it,

_____

no _____ !

Phonics Practice

Silent Consonants

Write the word to complete each sentence.

bought   bright   sight

_____

1. The sailors set out on a _____ sunny day.

knew   know   knock

_____

2. Sailors must _____ a lot about ships.

knots   knife   knew

_____

3. They must be able to tie _____ .

wrote   wrist   wrong

_____

4. Sailors must know if something is _____ with the ship.

fight   might   many

_____

5. When I grow up, I _____ decide to be a sailor.

Name _____

Extra Phonics Practice

© Scott, Foresman and Company   G2

Buffy's Orange Leash   Practice Book 197

R-Controlled Vowels er, ir, ur

Name the picture in each box. Circle the word that has the same vowel sound as the picture.

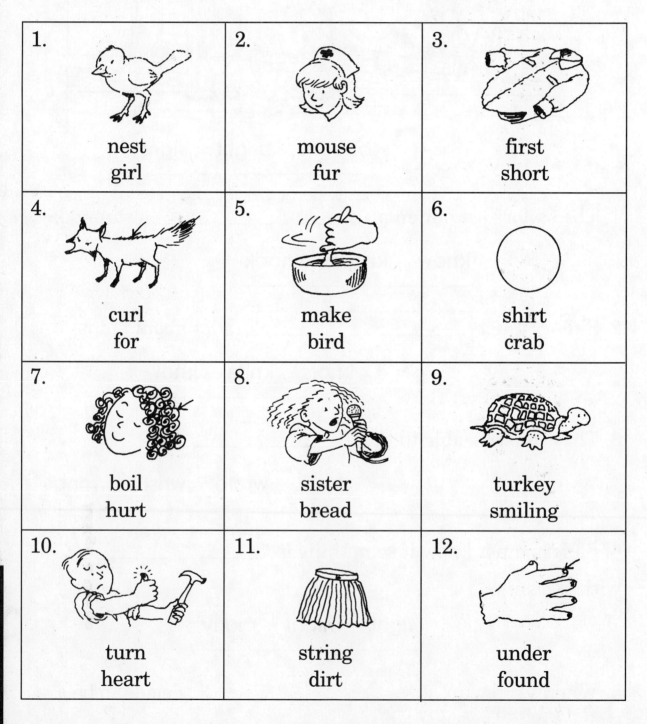

1. nest girl	**2.** mouse fur	**3.** first short
4. curl for	**5.** make bird	**6.** shirt crab
7. boil hurt	**8.** sister bread	**9.** turkey smiling
10. turn heart	**11.** string dirt	**12.** under found

Buffy's Orange Leash

Theme Log

Literature	What I Learned About the Theme	How I Liked the Literature Assign a Grade
Soccer Sam		A B C D F
Nessa's Fish		A B C D F
With the Wind		A B C D F
Minnie the Mambo Mosquito		A B C D F
Gino Badino		A B C D F
Slippery Ice		A B C D F
Higher on the Door		A B C D F
Additional Reading		A B C D F
		A B C D F

Vocabulary

These words can describe a game like basketball or soccer.
Write anything you might know about each word. Use your
glossary if you need help.

introduce

---

dribbling

---

practiced

Write a sentence about a game. Use at least one of the
vocabulary words from above in your sentence.

Independent Reading Guide

Before You Read

❏ **Preview and Predict:** Look at the pictures in the story. Which boy is Sam? How do you think he earns the nickname "Soccer Sam"?

As You Read

❏ **Pages 6 to 11:** Read to find out why Sam is embarrassed and Marco is unhappy. Do you think Sam and Marco will learn to understand each other?

❏ **Pages 12 to 19:** What brings Marco, Sam, and the second-grade class together as friends? How does Sam challenge the third graders? Read on to find out.

❏ **Pages 20 to 26:** Do you think the second graders can win over the third graders? Read to find out who wins and how Sam becomes "Soccer Sam."

After You Read

❏ Draw or write about your favorite part of the story.

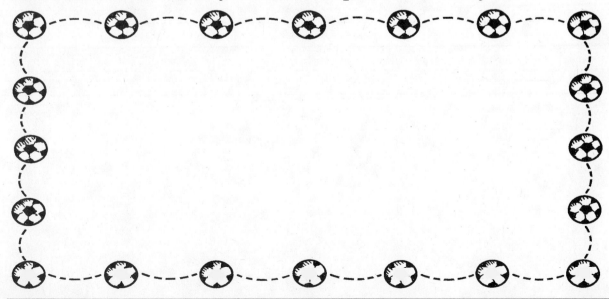

Comprehension Check

1. How do you think Marco will feel now about living with Sam? Tell why you think that way.

_____

_____

_____

2. Describe what Sam is like.

_____

_____

_____

3. How do you think the third graders will treat the second graders now? Explain.

_____

_____

_____

Cause and Effect

Read these WHY questions from *Soccer Sam*. Tell why they happened.

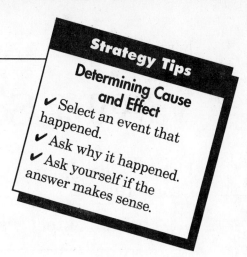

Pages	WHY Question—Effect	Answer—Cause
8–9	Why did the kids laugh at Marco?	
10	Why did Marco and Sam leave?	
12	Why did Sam's mother, Sam, and Marco go to the mall?	
13	Why did they buy a soccer ball?	
18	Why did the third graders laugh at the second graders?	
24	Why did the second graders win the game?	

Variable Sounds for oo

Use the words in the box. Label the picture.

books   stool   scoop   boots   broom   hooks   spoons

Soccer Sam

Variable Sounds for oo

Underline all the words in the story that have the sound you hear in *fool* or *hood*.

Maria and Kristy went to summer camp. They swam in the pool every day. At lunch they had good food. Sometimes they cooked out. The children took turns with chores. Maria stooped to pick up a tool. Kristy stood on a stool to clean. Others gathered wood. Everyone worked hard and had fun.

Write the underlined words below the word with the same vowel sound.

fool	**hood**

Extra Phonics Practice

Silent Consonants

Use the words in the box. Write the word that makes sense in each sentence.

write	know	neighbor	wrote	knock

_____
----
1. My aunt _____ me a letter.

_____
----
2. I sat down to _____ back to her.

_____
----
3. I heard a _____ at the door.

_____
----
4. I knew it was my _____ , Rob.

5. We had fun looking at old photographs of _____
----
people we _____ .

Soccer Sam

Vocabulary

These words are from *Nessa's Fish*. How much do you know about these words? Put an X below your answer.

Word	I know what this word means.	I have seen or heard this word.	I don't know what this word means.
dashed			
inland			
loped			
shivered			
shuffled			

Now use two of the vocabulary words you know in a sentence. Remember to check your glossary for words you are unsure about.

_____

_____

_____

_____

_____

_____

Independent Reading Guide

Before You Read

❑ **Preview and Predict:** Where does the story take place? Is it cold there? hot? Is it near where you live? How do you know? What are the clues? Would you like to live there?

As You Read

❑ **Pages 28 to 33:** Read to find out what happens to Nessa and her grandmother while they are on a fishing trip.

❑ **Pages 34 to 41:** What should you do if you meet a pack of wolves? What should you NOT do if you meet a wild bear? Find out what Nessa does.

❑ **Pages 42 to 44:** "The moon watched over them all until a noise awakened Nessa." What is the noise? Are Nessa and her grandmother saved? Find out what happens to Nessa, her grandmother, and the fish.

After You Read

❑ Write a Survival Guide. It should contain information about what you should and should not do if you meet a fox, a wolf, and a bear. Add other animals if you choose.

Comprehension Check

1. Why do you think the animals listen to Nessa?

_____

- -

_____

- -

_____

2. If you were Nessa, would you be frightened? Tell why or why not.

_____

- -

_____

- -

_____

3. Write down what Nessa's parents might say to her when they find out what happened.

_____

- -

_____

- -

_____

- -

_____

Draw Conclusions

Reread page 36 of *Nessa's Fish* and explain
Nessa's actions when she meets the bear.

Nessa's Actions	Why?

Nessa's Fish

Less Common Vowels

Write the words that make sense in the story.
Write an ending to the story on another piece of paper.

fall   fin   **taught   tot**

1. One _____ day, Sue _____
Jill how to fish.

ill   all

2. They fished _____ afternoon.

caught   cat

3. They _____ big fish

small   smile

and _____ fish.

mark   almost

4. When it was _____ dark,
they packed up their gear to go home.

saw   sow

5. Suddenly they _____ a wolf.
They knew what to do.

Phonics Practice

Less Common Vowels

Circle one word in each sentence that has the same vowel sound as *haul, ball,* and *draw.*

1. Grandpa taught Liz how to help.

2. The people were ready for the balloon launch.

3. After Liz caught the rope, she held it tight.

4. She saw many interesting sights from the balloon.

5. The children on the team ran past all the people.

6. The children are tall and very quick.

Nessa's Fish

Extra Phonics Practice

Variable Sounds for oo

Underline all the words in the story that have the sound you hear in *boom* or *hood*.

It was about noon when the Tell family drove into their campground. Dad announced, "Look! We're here!"

"I'm ready for some good food!' cried Karl.

"Well, first we need to set up the tent and chop some wood so we can cook," said Mom.

Karl grabbed a tool to pound in the tent stakes. Emmie took a broom to sweep out the tent.

"We'll be done in no time with all your help," said Mom. "Then we can all go to the pool!"

After a fun-filled day, they sat in front of their fire and ate their dinner.

Write the underlined words below the word with the same vowel sound.

boom	**hood**

Vocabulary

These words are from *With the Wind*. How much do you know about these words? Put an X below your answer.

Word	I know what this word means.	I have seen or heard this word.	I don't know what this word means.
creature			
among			
freedom			
hooves			
strength			
strengthening			

Now use two of the vocabulary words you know in a sentence. Remember to check your glossary for words you are unsure about.

Independent Reading Guide

Before You Read

❑ **Preview and Predict:** Look at the pictures on pages 48–49. What do you think this poem is about? Who are the main characters in the poem?

As You Read

❑ **Pages 48 to 55:** As you read, take notes about how the boy feels when he rides a horse.

TIP!
☞ Look at the pictures carefully as you read to find out what is special about the boy in the poem.

❑ **Pages 56 to 62:** Read to find out why the boy feels "strong" when he rides the horse.

After You Read

❑ What makes you feel "strong"? One example might be riding a bicycle. Draw a picture of yourself doing something that makes you feel "strong" like the boy in the poem.

Comprehension Check

Draw a picture that shows how the boy feels when he rides horseback. Then tell why he feels that way.

With the Wind

Compare and Contrast

Picture your experiences and the boy's
experiences in *With the Wind*.
Draw them both here.

My experiences:

The boy's experiences:

Diphthongs ou, ow

Write the words that make sense in the story.

outdoors   water
_____

1. The boy loved being _____ .

toy   town
_____

2. He rode through the _____ ,

hale   houses
_____

past the _____ ,

flowers   flaws
_____

and past the _____ .

down   desk
_____

3. He rode _____

air   around
_____

the hill and _____ the lake.

different   down
_____

4. He lay _____ in the shade

clowned   counted   **clouds   clop**
_____   _____

and _____ the _____ .

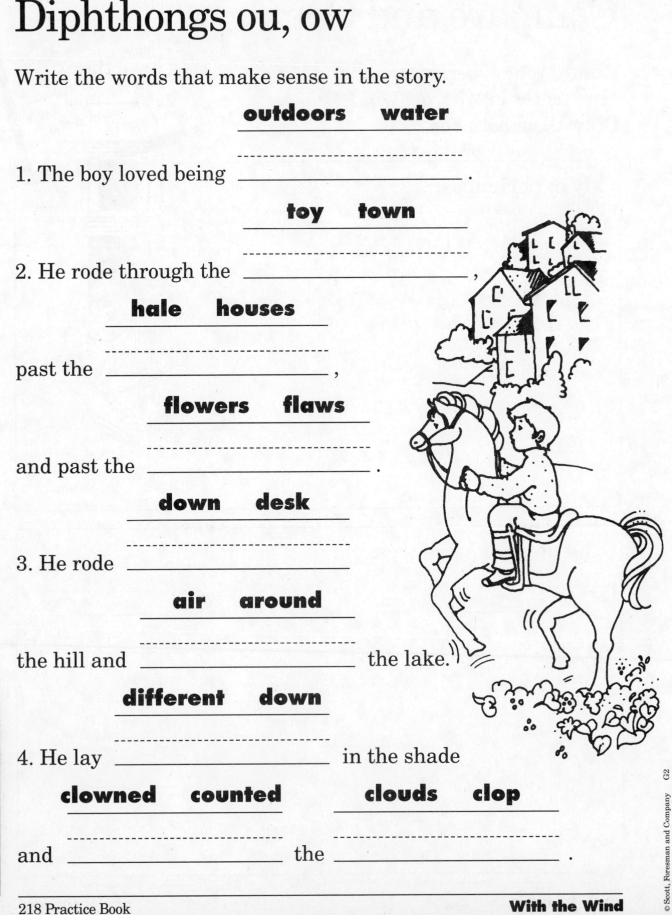

© Scott, Foresman and Company   G2

With the Wind

Phonics Practice

Diphthongs ou, ow

Circle three words in each set of sentences that have the same vowel sound as *cloud* and *brown*.

Brian brought some wood to the back of the house. He put the wood down on the ground.

He started to pound with his hammer. The loud noise made him frown.

He sanded and painted the rough wood. He built a yellow castle. He shouted about it because he was so proud.

Write the words you circled on the lines below.

1. _____   2. _____   3. _____

4. _____   5. _____   6. _____

7. _____   8. _____   9. _____

With the Wind

Extra Phonics Practice

Verb Endings -ing

Write the word that makes sense in each sentence.

helped   helping
_____

1. I am _____ Dad water the flowers.

picked   picking
_____

2. We are also _____ some flowers for Mom.

play   playing
_____

3. Soon we will _____ a game.

Write each word without its ending.

4. helping

_____

_____

5. picking

_____

_____

6. playing

_____

_____

© Scott, Foresman and Company   G2

Phonics Review

With the Wind

Animal Fantasy

Complete after reading *Minnie the Mambo Mosquito* and *Gino Badino.*

Minnie is a mosquito. What other kinds of animals have been used as fantasy characters in stories you've read?

Gino Badino is part of an animal family. They all work together to do the same sorts of things most families do. What things do they do that are like your family, and what things are different?

T **ry one of these ideas:**
- Animal fantasies always include animals as characters, but they can take place in a real place or in a make-believe place. Tell about some real places Minnie the Mambo Mosquito or Gino Badino might find themselves in their next books.
- Both Minnie and Gino are animals that wear clothes. Draw a picture of your favorite animal wearing clothes. Save the picture for later as a story starter.

Minnie the Mambo Mosquito

Genre Study

Vocabulary

Draw a picture to explain the meaning of each word. Use your glossary if you are unsure about a word's meaning.

dive-bombing

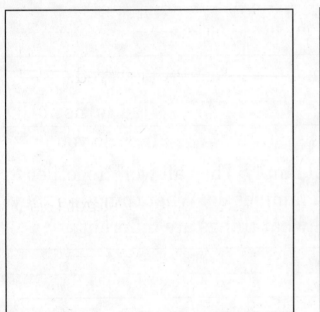

radio

mosquito

Minnie the Mambo Mosquito

Independent Reading Guide

Before You Read

❏ **Preview and Predict:** Why do you think Minnie is called the "Mambo Mosquito"? What do you know about mosquitoes? How do you think Minnie might be different from other mosquitoes?

As You Read

❏ **Pages 64 to 67:** Read to find out why Minnie liked Fred.

❏ **Pages 68 to 71:** Find out what happens when Fred turns off his radio! Will Minnie and Fred still be friends? What do you think will happen?

❏ **Pages 72 to 74:** Read to find out how the author first got the idea for a story about a mosquito.

After You Read

❏ Draw two words that look like they sound. One example has been done for you.

Comprehension Check

1. Do you think Minnie is happy that she didn't bite Fred? Tell why or why not.

_____

_____

_____

2. What do you think the other mosquitoes would say about Minnie?

_____

_____

_____

3. Do you think Fred knows Minnie dances to the music on his radio? Explain why you think that way.

_____

_____

_____

Minnie the Mambo Mosquito

Plot

Consider the following:

Strategy Ti

Understanding Plot
✔ Predict how characters will act.
✔ What do characters say, do, and think? What do you think they'll do next?
✔ Keep reading to see if you are right.

What I Know About Mosquitoes	What I Know About Minnie	What I Know About Fred

Predictions:

Variable Sounds for ou

Use the words in the box.
Write the words to complete the poem.

| pounce | about | thought | house | out | ought |

Bug Thoughts

1. Here's a thought
perhaps we ought
_____

----
to think _____ :

2. People pounce on bugs
As if to announce,
_____

"You're in my _____ !
_____

You must stay _____ !"
_____

----
3. Bugs _____ on people

As if to announce,
"You're in my house! You must stay in!"
_____

----
4. Yes, there's a _____
_____

----
perhaps we _____ to think about.

Phonics Practice

226 Practice Book

Minnie the Mambo Mosquito

© Scott, Foresman and Company   G2

Variable Sounds for ou

Circle one word in each sentence that has the same vowel sound as *cough*.

1. Carlos thought about what he should bring back from his trip.

2. He brought back four round balloons for his friends.

Circle one word in each sentence that has the same vowel sound as *cloud*.

3. Something always smells good at Mr. Wood's house.

4. When I visited last Tuesday, I asked him about the soup he was cooking.

5. Mr. Wood said he would be proud to let me help him make the soup.

6. After the soup was ready, Mr. Wood said, "Try the soup before it gets cold, but don't burn your mouth!"

Long o

Circle the words in the box that have the same vowel sound
as *rope*.

sky	woke	home	spoke	note

Write the words to complete the sentences.

1. The squirrel makes her

_____

_____ in a tree.

_____

----

2. The noisy birds _____
the man.

_____

----

3. I will write a _____ to
my friend.

_____

----

4. Mom _____ to the new
neighbors.

Minnie the Mambo Mosquito

Vocabulary

The following questions include words that you will find in *Gino Badino.* You may need to use your glossary to answer these questions.

1. What can you make out of *dough?*

_____

- -

_____

2. Have you ever *molded* anything out of clay or dough? What did you make?

_____

- -

_____

3. Have you ever *discarded* anything? What did you discard?

_____

- -

_____

4. Ask a question using each of these words. Use your glossary for help.

macaroni

_____

- -

_____

explosion

_____

- -

_____

G2

Independent Reading Guide

Before You Read

❑ **Preview and Predict:** Read the title and look at the pictures. Which character is Gino? The mice in the story are very busy. What do you think they are doing?

As You Read

❑ **Pages 76 to 85:** Find out how Gino changes a job he hates into fun! How does Gino's father feel about Gino's fun?

TIP! Notice how the animal characters think and act like people.

❑ **Pages 86 to 92:** Read on to find out what happens when Gino tries to help out with the family business.

❑ **Pages 93 to 96:** Will the big mistake be found out? What do you think will happen to Gino Badino?

After You Read

❑ Make up an ad for Badino pasta.

G2

Comprehension Check

1. Would this story be different if Gino did not try to make pasta by himself?

_____
_____
_____
_____
_____
_____

2. Tell how you think Gino's family will treat him now.

_____
_____
_____
_____
_____
_____

3. Do you think you and Gino are alike? Tell why or why not.

_____
_____
_____
_____
_____
_____

Identify Problems

Read each page from *Gino Badino*. Identify problem spots. Write them down. Think of strategies you can use to help. Write them down.

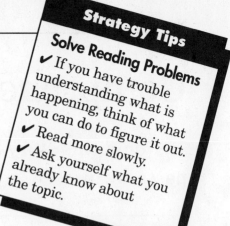

Page 91	**Trouble Spots:**
	How I Figured It Out:

Page 93	**Trouble Spots:**
	How I Figured It Out:

Page 95	**Trouble Spots:**
	How I Figured It Out:

Gino Badino

Diphthongs oi, oy

Use the words in the box. Write the answers to the riddles. There is one extra word. Write your own riddle about it.

boy   point   voice   toys   noisy   coins

1. If something is very loud, it is ____.

_____

2. If you are not a girl, you're a ____.

_____

3. What do you use when you talk?

_____

4. What's at the end of a pin?

_____

5. Pennies, nickels, dimes, and quarters are ____.

_____

6. Write your own riddle using the extra word.

_____

_____

_____

_____

_____

G2

Gino Badino

Diphthongs oi, oy

Circle three words in each set of sentences that have the same vowel sound as *foil* and *toy*.

Roy liked to play ball with the other boys and girls on the team. He did not hear the noise of the crowd.

He jumped for joy because he made two points. The crowd grew very noisy.

Some of the fans raised their voices in a cheer. Other fans joined in and clapped. Everyone there enjoyed the game.

Write the words you circled on the lines below.

1. _____ 2. _____ 3. _____

4. _____ 5. _____ 6. _____

7. _____ 8. _____ 9. _____

Gino Badino

Vowels ou, ow

Say the first word in the row. Circle the word that has the same vowel sound.

1. cow	snow	shake	gown
2. loud	drop	sock	found
3. town	sound	braid	block
4. loud	how	boy	tone
5. house	stop	shout	coat
6. clown	most	crowd	think
7. mouth	clock	toy	crown
8. shout	chop	brow	mop
9. down	show	south	broke
10. brown	stove	could	owl

Gino Badino

Vocabulary

These words can describe ice. Write anything you might know about each word. Use your glossary if you need help.

iceberg

_____
- -
_____

edge

_____
- -
_____
- -
_____

slippery

_____
- -
_____

Write a sentence about ice. Use at least one of the words above in your sentence.

_____
- -
_____
- -
_____
- -
_____

Slippery Ice

Independent Reading Guide

Before You Read

❑ **Preview and Predict:** Where does the story take place? Who are the main characters in the story? What are the penguins' names? Which ones rhyme? Which is the best name for a penguin? Which is your favorite?

As You Read

❑ **Pages 98 to 105:** Find out what problem the penguins are having.

❑ **Pages 106 to 108:** Do the penguins end up in the water? Find out how the story ends.

TIP!
☞ Notice how the pictures show how slippery the ice is for the penguins.

After You Read

❑ Add your own ending to the story. Finish the story by telling how the penguins got back up on the iceberg.

Comprehension Check

1. How do you think the penguins feel when they fall in the water? Tell why you think that way.

_____

- -

_____

- -

_____

2. Do you think the penguins like living on the iceberg? Explain why or why not.

_____

- -

_____

- -

_____

3. Tell one way these penguins are like real penguins and one way they are different.

_____

- -

_____

- -

_____

- -

_____

Slippery Ice

Cause and Effect

Strategy Tips

Cause and Effect

✔ Think about each event in the story. Why did it happen?

✔ Does one thing cause another to happen?

✔ As you read, think: What will happen next?

Write about something that you predicted would happen in *Slippery Ice*. Tell why. Then write what really happened.

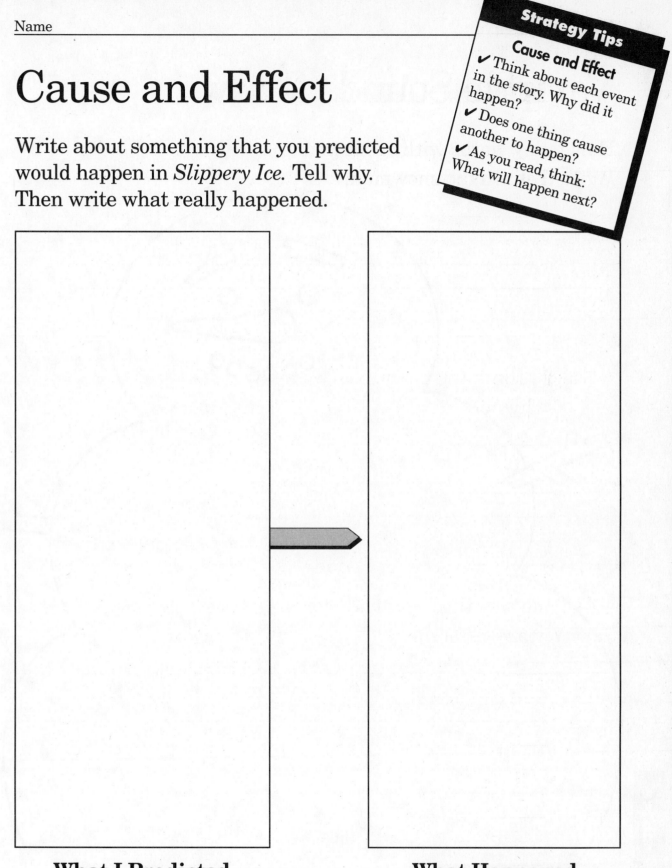

What I Predicted   **What Happened**

Variable Sounds for ow

How many words with *ow* do you know?
Write them in the snowman.

© Scott, Foresman and Company   G2

Slippery Ice

Variable Sounds for ow

Write the letters *ow* to make a word. Then read each word.

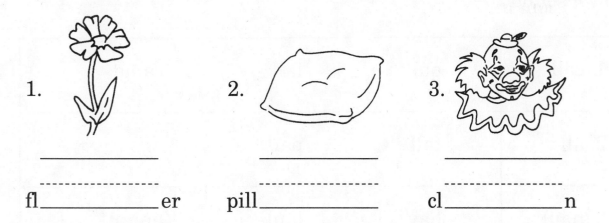

1. _____

fl_____er

2. _____

pill_____

3. _____

cl_____n

Write a word from above to complete each sentence.

4. The _____ did tricks that made us laugh.

5. A nice, soft _____ can help you sleep.

6. The purple _____ was the tallest
in the garden.

Extra Phonics Practice

Vowels au, aw, all

Say the first word in the row. Circle the word that has the same vowel sound.

1. call	quill	fall	came
2. all	tall	pail	age
3. haul	hay	hail	haunt
4. claw	frown	small	snail
5. straw	said	stay	shawl
6. walk	lawn	become	game
7. ball	badge	pause	cave
8. launch	arm	fault	chain
9. salt	talk	sail	save
10. draw	drain	take	bald

Slippery Ice

Compare and Contrast

Read each head on the chart.
Fill in the rest of the chart.

Strategy Tips

Compare and Contrast

✔ Think about what the character does and says.
✔ Compare your own experiences with the character's experiences.
✔ How are you and the character alike? How are you different?

Ways I am like or different from Mr. Stevenson	How my experiences can help me understand Mr. Stevenson

Less Common Vowels

Use the words in the box. Write the words to complete the sentences. Then answer the question at the bottom of the page.

| eight   father's   pudding   pushed   neighbors |

When Lisa was small, she liked to

_____

eat _____ ,

_____

ride on her _____

shoulders, _____

visit with her _____ ,

_____

be _____ on the swing, and

_____

count to _____ .

What did you like to do when you were small?

_____

_____

_____

_____

G2

Higher on the Door

Less Common Vowels

Use the words in the box.
Write the words to complete the story.

pulled	bushes	sleigh	Father	eight	palm	neigh

It was a beautiful winter day. Snow stuck to

_____

the _____ and trees.

_____

_____ took us for

_____

a _____ ride. I could hear

_____

the horses _____ as we reached the stable.

_____

Two horses _____

_____

all _____ of us. After the ride, a horse ate

_____

sugar from the _____ of my hand.

Variable Sounds for ow

Circle one word in each sentence that has the same vowel sound as *show*.

1. The town and the fields near it were white with snow.

2. A bird flew low over the ground looking at the field.

3. "I know there is food in that field," it said.

Circle one word in each sentence that has the same vowel sound as *crown*.

4. The bird began to slow down to stop on a branch.

5. "I think I'll go to town," it said. "A little boy lives there who gives me seeds."

Phonics Review

Higher on the Door

© Scott, Foresman and Company G2

Picture Graph

Select a topic.

List heads.

Decide on five entries.

Choose a picture.

Take a vote of everyone in the class.

Draw a picture for each vote.

Title

Heads

Entries

Study Skills

My Ideas

Theme Log

Literature	What I Learned About the Theme	How I Liked the Literature
My Dog Is Lost!		🖐 🖐
The Lost Lake		🖐 🖐
Dinosaurs on the Road		🖐 🖐
Dinosaurs, Dragonflies & Diamonds: All About Natural History Museums		🖐 🖐
Planet of the Grown-Ups		🖐 🖐
The Tub People		🖐 🖐
Additional Reading		🖐 🖐
		🖐 🖐
		🖐 🖐

Rating Scale

🖐 liked   🖐 did not like

Vocabulary

Follow the directions to write newspaper headlines using the words from *My Dog Is Lost*. Remember to use your glossary for words you are not sure about.

1. Use the words *search* and *shaggy* in a headline about a lost dog.

_____

_____

_____

_____

2. Use the words *lonelier* and *miserable* in a headline about a boy whose best friend just moved away.

_____

_____

_____

_____

3. Use the word *language* in a headline about a dog who understands different languages.

_____

_____

_____

_____

My Dog Is Lost!

Independent Reading Guide

Before You Read

❏ **Preview and Predict:** Read the title and look at the pictures. What has happened to the boy? How do you think he feels?

As You Read

❏ **Pages 6 to 13:** Where is Pepito? As you read, use the street map to follow the trail of Juanito's search for Pepito.

❏ **Pages 14 to 27:** Continue the search for Pepito. Add to the map as you read.

❏ **Pages 28 to 33:** Find out if Juanito finds Pepito. What does Juanito find as he searches for his dog?

After You Read

❏ Write a description of someone in your class. Trade papers with a partner. See if your partner can guess the name of the person you described.

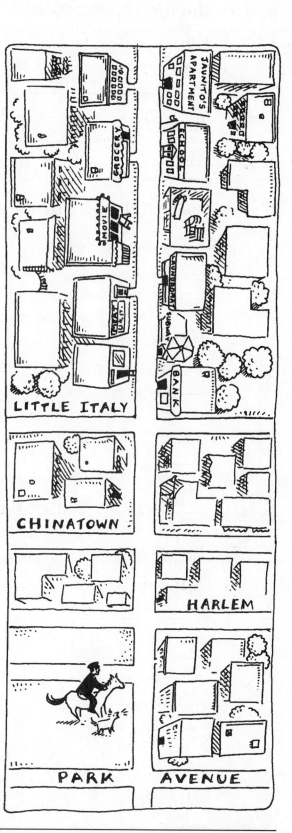

My Dog Is Lost!

Comprehension Check

1. How do you think Pepito felt while he was lost? Tell why.

_____

_____

_____

2. Describe what you think Juanito is like.

_____

_____

_____

_____

3. How do you think Juanito will feel now about living in New York City? Tell why you think that way.

_____

_____

_____

My Dog Is Lost!

Fix-up Strategies: Glossary

Choose five words from *My Dog Is Lost!*
Put them in alphabetical order. Draw
pictures to show what the words mean.

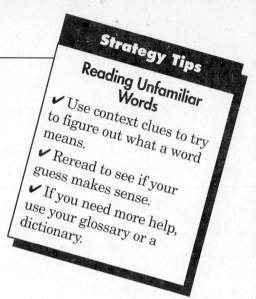

Comparatives and Superlatives

Add -er or -est to the words below.
Remember to change final *y* to *i* if you need to.

smart
_____

1. "Dogs are _____ than cats," said Liz.

smart
_____

2. "Cats are _____ than dogs," said Meg.

friendly
_____

3. "Dogs are _____ than cats,"
said Liz.

easy
_____

4. "Cats are _____ to take care of than dogs,"
said Meg.

funny
_____

5. "Your cat is the _____ cat I know,"
said Liz.

happy
_____

6. "Your dog is the _____ dog I know,"
said Meg.

"It's a good thing we're sisters," said Liz. "We can share
our pets!"

Phonics Practice

My Dog Is Lost!

Comparatives and Superlatives

Circle the word that makes sense in each sentence.

1. The sky is ____ in the morning than at night.

   lightest   light   lighter

2. Of all the players on the team, Dad was the ____.

   fast   fastest   faster

3. The pine tree is ____ than the house.

   taller   tall   tallest

4. Jane is the ____ of all the children.

   old   oldest   older

5. This lake is ____ than the pond.

   deepest   deep   deeper

6. The ducks fly ____ than the bees.

   higher   high   highest

7. Last Saturday was the ____ day of the year.

   colder   coldest   cold

Extra Phonics Practice

Contractions

Use the contractions in the box. Write the contraction that goes with each pair of words.

We're	I'm	You've	It's

It is _____   We are _____

_____   _____

I am _____   You have _____

Write the contraction to complete each sentence.

1. Everyone in my family works with

_____

our dog Red. _____ all
training him.

_____

2. _____ training Red to
play ball.

3. Red is learning fast!

_____

_____ never seen a more
clever dog.

My Dog Is Lost!

G2

Phonics Review

Vocabulary

These words can describe a hike. Use each word in a
sentence about a hike. Use your glossary if you need help.

backpack

_____

_____

compass

_____

_____

gasping

_____

_____

hikers

_____

_____

hiking

_____

_____

knapsack

_____

_____

outdoorsmen

_____

_____

Independent Reading Guide

Before You Read

❑ **Preview and Predict:** Who are the main characters in the story? Where does the story begin? Where are the characters at the end of the story? How can a lake be lost?

As You Read

❑ **Pages 36 to 40:** Read about how some old magazine pictures change a summer vacation from dull to exciting.

❑ **Pages 41 to 43:** What surprise does Dad plan for Luke? What happens when they arrive at Lost Lake?

❑ **Pages 44 to 52:** Read to find out if Luke and Dad find their own lost lake.

After You Read

❑ Compare and contrast how Dad and Luke acted in the city to how they acted on the camping trip.

TIP! Notice how the characters change as the setting changes.

	City	Camping Trip
Dad		
Luke		

G2

The Lost Lake

Comprehension Check

1. Do you think Luke ever went camping before? Tell why you think that way.

_____

_____

_____

_____

2. Do you think Luke's father enjoyed the camping trip? Tell why or why not.

_____

_____

_____

_____

3. How do you think Luke and his dad will get along after their camping trip? Explain.

_____

_____

_____

_____

Setting

Describe how Luke's dad's feelings change in different settings in *The Lost Lake*.

Place	What It Is Like	How Dad Acts and Feels
Dad's apartment in the city		
at the Lost Lake		
in the tent on the first night		
at their second campsite		

Suffixes -ful, -ly

Add *-ful* or *-ly* to the words
below so they make sense
in the story.

Dad and I went on a hike.

_____
- - - - - - - - - - - - - - - -
1. The fall trees were color_____ .

_____
- - - - - - - - - - - - - - - -
2. We were care_____ not to litter.

_____
- - - - - - - - - - - - - - - -
3. We walked quiet_____ so we wouldn't
bother any animals.

_____
- - - - - - - - - - - - - - - -
4. Walking sticks were help_____ when we
walked up a hill.

_____
- - - - - - - - - - - - - - - -
5. The ducks were real_____ noisy as they
flew by.

_____
- - - - - - - - - - - - - - - -
6. It was a wonder_____ afternoon.

Phonics Practice

Suffixes -ful, -ly

Add a word from the box to each suffix to make new words that make sense in the sentences.

| love   thank   care   perfect   neat |

1. It's a _____ ly
   _____
   day for a picnic.

2. Be _____ ful not to
   _____
   let the eggs fall.

3. Put the food _____ ly
   _____
   into the basket.

4. This is a _____ ly beautiful spot.
   _____

5. We can be _____ ful for such a
   _____
   nice day.

The Lost Lake

Extra Phonics Practice

Double Medial Consonants

Underline the word that makes sense in each sentence.

1. Each day the frog would _____ his friend, the duck, to the pond.

   follow   **middle**   **giggle**

2. Then the two would swim to the _____ of the pond.

   yellow   **follow**   **middle**

3. If they saw any of their friends at the pond, they would say _____ .

   yellow   **follow**   **hello**

4. Sometimes the frog would tell jokes that made the duck _____ .

   middle   **yellow**   **giggle**

5. The two friends would float all day together under the hot, _____ sun.

   yellow   **middle**   **giggle**

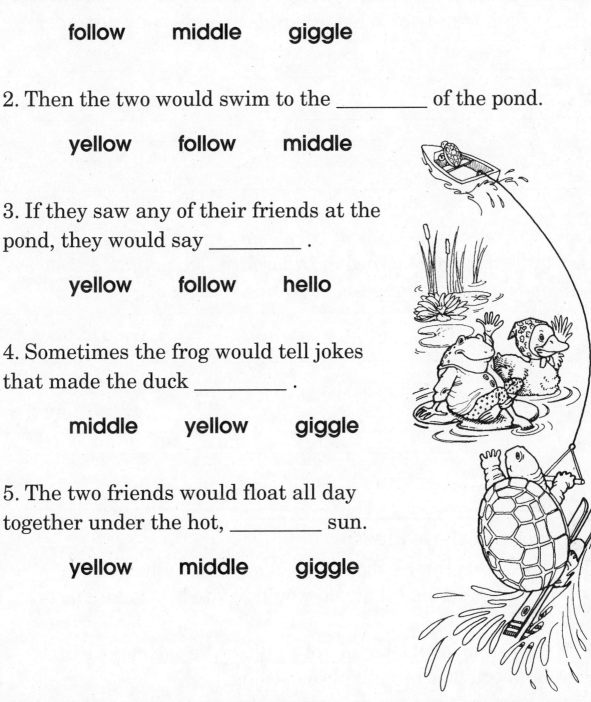

© Scott, Foresman and Company   G2

Phonics Review

Nonfiction

Complete after reading "Dinosaurs on the Road" and *Dinosaurs, Dragonflies & Diamonds.*

Headings are included in nonfiction to help you find information. In "Dinosaurs on the Road" where would you look to find out what to pack for a trip? What other ideas could you add under that heading?

_____

_____

_____

_____

Nonfiction tells us facts about people, animals, or things. List at least three facts you learned in *Dinosaurs, Dragonflies & Diamonds* and "Learning About Natural History."

_____

_____

_____

_____

_____

_____

T ry one of these ideas:

1. Nonfiction can be about almost any topic. Share three topics with a friend that you would like to learn more facts about.

2. Draw and label a picture of a bike. Save the picture to remind you how to explain something.

Dinosaurs on the Road

Vocabulary

The following questions include words that you will find in "Dinosaurs on the Road." You may need to use your glossary to answer these questions.

1. What kinds of *sights* do *travelers* like to see?

_____

- -

_____

2. What can a *conductor* do for *passengers* on a *subway*?

_____

- -

_____

3. Which do you think is more of an *adventure*—going fast on *skateboards* or going down *rapids* in a boat?

_____

- -

_____

4. Ask a question using each of these words. Use your glossary for help.

ferryboats

- -

_____

station

- -

_____

Independent Reading Guide

Before You Read

❏ **Preview and Predict:** Look at the pages of the story. Do you think the story will be funny, give facts, or both?

As You Read

❏ **Pages 56 to 60:** Read about how to prepare for a trip. If you could travel anywhere you'd like, where would you go?

❏ **Pages 61 to 74:** Read about different ways to travel. Draw a picture of your favorite way to travel. Which would you like to try?

❏ **Pages 75 to 76:** Read on to find out why traveling is an adventure.

After You Read

❏ Make a Travel Guide for Kids. Give some important tips to someone your age who is about to take a trip.

Comprehension Check

1. When you travel, why do you think it's important to pack only a few things?

_____

_____

_____

_____

2. "Dinosaurs on the Road" talks about many different ways to travel. Tell which way sounds best to you, and why.

_____

_____

_____

_____

_____

_____

3. Why do you think the illustrator used dinosaurs instead of people in the pictures for this selection?

_____

_____

_____

_____

Predict from Previewing

Write the page number and the titles or heads. Tell what the pictures show. Make a prediction.

Title/Headings	Pictures	What I Predict

Dinosaurs on the Road

R-Controlled Vowels -ar, -air

Use the words in the box. Write the words to complete the story. Answer the question at the bottom of the page.

pair	shared	airport	fare	scared	parents

1. Sue and her _____ took a trip to the mountains.

2. Sue packed a _____ of boots for hiking.

3. To get to the mountains, they paid a _____ to ride a train.

4. The train took them to the _____ .

5. On the plane, Sue _____ the window with her mom.

6. Sue wasn't _____ at all. She liked flying.

7. Where would you go if you could take a trip?

_____

_____

Phonics Practice

R-Controlled Vowels ar, air

Use the words in the box. Write the words that make sense in the story.

| chairs | pair | square | hair | glare | air | fair |

On a hot summer day,
Mom took Melissa and me to the beach.

_____

We took a big _____

blanket and folding _____ .

The sun's _____ bothered Mom's eyes so she put

on a _____ of sunglasses.

After lunch, we walked to the _____

at the other end of the beach. My _____ blew in the
breeze while I rode on the rides.

It felt good to be out in the warm

summer _____ . We had a wonderful day.

Dinosaurs on the Road

Comparatives and Superlatives

Circle the word that makes sense in each sentence.

1. That cloud is the _____ one in the sky.

   darker   dark   darkest

2. Grandpa's house is _____ than our house.

   small   smaller   smallest

3. Brown Street is the _____ street in town.

   shorter   short   shortest

4. This lake is _____ than the pond.

   cleaner   cleanest   clean

5. The frog jumped _____ than the toad.

   highest   higher   high

6. Sarah practiced _____ than I did on the recorder.

   longer   longest   long

7. That was the _____ story you ever told.

   great   greater   greatest

Phonics Review

Check for Meaning

Circle the correct meaning for the underlined word in the senetnce. Then draw a picture to go with each sentence.

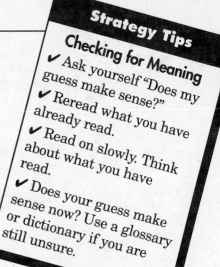

1. Angie showed me her new <u>bat</u>. She hit a home run with it in the game.

   a baseball bat   **a flying animal**

2. He passed out cups of <u>punch</u> at the party. It was red and very sweet.

   a fruit juice drink   **to hit with your fist**

3. We heard a loud <u>bark</u>. Our dog Jimmy had seen a squirrel.

   the outer part of a tree   **the noise a dog makes**

Dinosaurs, Dragonflies & Diamonds

Suffixes -ness, -less

Add *-ness* or *-less* to the words below
so they make sense in the story.

One day, a baby triceratops

_____
....

was care_____ and

wandered too far away from the herd.

Suddenly, the baby triceratops heard a terrible

_____
....

noise. It was the fear_____ tyrannosaurus.

_____
....

With surprising quick_____ , the triceratops

dashed away. He ran and ran, but the huge tyrannosaurus

_____
....

was tire_____ . For a while,

_____
....

it seemed hope_____ . Finally,

the triceratops saw a small cave. He raced inside and

_____
....

the dark_____ hid him from the tyrannosaurus.
He was safe.

Dinosaurs, Dragonflies & Diamonds

Phonics Practice

Suffixes -ness, -less

Add -less to each underlined word to make a new word.
Remember to change *y* to *i* if you need to.

1. Brian likes to <u>help</u> his baby brother eat.

   _____

   A _____ baby is so cute.

2. The old building doesn't show its <u>age</u>.

   _____

   It appears to be _____ .

3. This broken dish is not <u>worth</u> much.

   _____

   It is probably _____ .

Add -ness to each underlined word to make a new word.

4. The clouds are getting very <u>dark</u>.

   _____

   The _____ means it may rain.

5. Mr. Valdez is a <u>kind</u> man.

   _____

   He treats all his neighbors with _____ .

6. Keiko is such a <u>happy</u> person.

   _____

   Her _____ makes everyone feel good.

Dinosaurs, Dragonflies & Diamonds

Prefix dis

Write the word that makes sense in each sentence.

disorder   reorder

---

1. Marco's room is in complete _____ .

liked   disliked

---

2. He _____
putting his toys away.

3. His mother was very

appointed   disappointed

_____ .

agreed   disagree

---

4. Finally, he _____
to clean up.

5. Marco made all the toys

appear   disappear

_____ by
putting them in the toy box.

approve   disapprove

---

6. His mother will _____ .

Phonics Review

Taking Notes

How We Learn About Life Long Ago

   You can see fossils in a natural history museum. Fossils tell about plants and animals of long ago. Fossils can be parts of plants and animals like bones. Fossils are also marks left by plants and animals. These parts or marks were often left in mud. The mud got hard and turned into rock after many years.
   Fossils show what kinds of plants and animals used to live on earth. Fossils show the size and shape of plants and animals.
   Fossils can also tell about what an animal ate. Pointed teeth tell that the animal ate meat. Animals with flat teeth ate mostly plants.

1. Read the selection and take notes on another piece of paper.

2. What is the selection about?

   _____

   _____

3. What are fossils?

   _____

   _____

4. What can people learn from fossils?

   _____

   _____

   _____

   _____

Dinosaurs, Dragonflies & Diamonds

Study Skills

Vocabulary

These words are from *Planet of the Grown-Ups*. How much do you know about these words? Put an X below your answer.

Word	I know what this word means.	I have seen or heard this word.	I don't know what this word means.
carnival			
computer			
expert			
grown-up			
planet			
props			
schedules			
special effects			

Now use two or more of the vocabulary words you know in a sentence. Remember to check your glossary for words you are unsure about.

_____

_____

_____

Independent Reading Guide

Before You Read

❑ **Preview and Predict:** Read the play, *Planet of the Grown-Ups*, with friends. Decide who will play the different characters. Gather the props. What materials would you need to do the special effects?

As You Read

❑ **Pages 102 to 107:** Where are Tasha, Louis, Pat, and Anna? How did they get there? Read about a computer program that can change children!

❑ **Pages 108 to 111:** What job does Tasha choose? Find out how she mixes everything up.

❑ **Pages 112 to 114:** Does Zegna repair the computer? Find out if the four friends get back home.

After You Read

❑ Write a skit about growing up. In your skit tell how you feel about growing up or what you'd like to be.

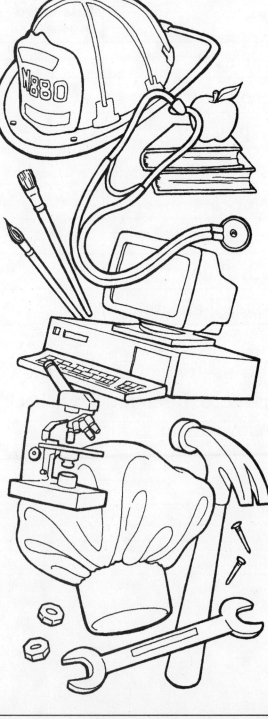

Planet of the Grown-Ups

Comprehension Check

1. If you were in trouble, would you like Tasha to help you? Tell why or why not.

_____

_____

_____

2. How do you think Zegna feels at the end of the story? Tell why.

_____

_____

_____

3. Do you think Zarlo would be a good place to live? Explain why you think that way.

_____

_____

_____

_____

Visualizing

Choose another selection to read. Visualize
to put yourself in the character's place.
How do you feel? What would you do?

Page	What Is Happening	How I Would Feel	What I Would Do

Adding Endings to Words with Final -y

Add *-es* or *-ed* to the words below.

Remember to change final *y* to *i* before you add the ending.

Dear Mom,

I'm a grown-up now on the planet Zarlo.

try

_____

I _____ to call you yesterday, but there
are no phones.

worry

_____

Don't be _____ about me because I got
a job building spaceships.

My robot is a big help.

carry

_____

He always _____ all the heavy parts.

hurry

_____

He _____ when there's a lot of work to do.

marry

_____

I'm getting _____ next week.
Can you come to the wedding?

Love,
Steve

Planet of the Grown-Ups

Adding Endings to Words with Final -y

Circle the word that makes sense in each sentence.

1. Every day a bird ____ to that branch to sing.

    flying   flies

2. Coughing has ____ my throat.

    dried   dries

3. The birds were upset by the cat's ____.

    cried   cries

4. Nick ____ the ball for a touchdown.

    carried   carrying

5. My little sister often ____ to read my books.

    trying   tries

Planet of the Grown-Ups

Suffix -ly

Write the word that makes sense in each sentence.

busy   busily
----

1. Akimi _____ planted her garden.

careful   carefully
----

2. She _____ placed
the plants in the ground.

quiet   quietly
----

3. She worked _____ .

recent   recently
----

4. It hadn't rained _____ ,
but she was hopeful.

final   finally
----

5. When she was _____

happy   happily
----

finished, she was _____ .

Phonics Review

Vocabulary

Draw a picture to explain the meaning of each word. Use your glossary if you are unsure about a word's meaning.

dizzier

drain

whirlpool

wink

The Tub People

Independent Reading Guide

Before You Read

❏ **Preview and Predict:** Is this story about something real or pretend? How can you tell?

As You Read

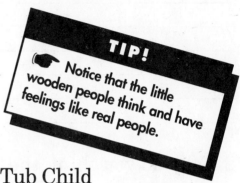

TIP!
Notice that the little wooden people think and have feelings like real people.

❏ **Pages 118 to 122:** Read about the adventures of the Tub People. What happens to Tub Child?

❏ **Pages 123 to 127:** What happens to Tub Child after he is rescued?

❏ **Pages 128 to 131:** Does Tub Child get back to his family? Read about the new adventures of the Tub People.

❏ **Pages 132 to 134:** Where did Pam Conrad get her ideas for the Tub People?

After You Read

❏ What toys do you have that are like the Tub People? What games do you play with them?

Comprehension Check

1. Describe how you think the Tub Child felt while he was stuck in the drain.

_____
- -
_____
_____
- -
_____

2. Why do you think the Tub People were moved from the bathtub to a bedroom?

_____
- -
_____
_____
- -
_____

3. Do the Tub People seem like real people to you? Tell why or why not.

_____
- -
_____
_____
- -
_____
_____
- -
_____

 © Scott, Foresman and Company   G2 **The Tub People**

Realism or Fantasy

Reread *Planet of the Grown-Ups*. Write
things that can happen in real life. Write
things that can happen only in fantasy.

Can Happen in Real Life	Can Happen Only in Fantasy

Endings -er, -en

Write the root word for each underlined word.
Then write an ending for the story.

_____

The little <u>wooden</u> people liked their new

\-\-\-\-\-\-\-\-\-\-\-\-\-\-\-\-

_____

home in the <u>silken</u> covers. The father was

_____

\-\-\-\-\-\-\-\-\-\-\-\-\-\-\-\-

a <u>painter</u>, so he painted the sheets. The

_____

\-\-\-\-\-\-\-\-\-\-\-\-\-\-\-\-

mother was a <u>farmer</u>, so she grew plants

_____

in the bed. The grandmother was the brave

_____

\-\-\-\-\-\-\-\-\-\-\-\-\-\-\-\-

<u>leader</u> of all the little people. One day, the

_____

big people came home early. She told them,

_____

\-\-\-\-\-\-\-\-\-\-\-\-\-\-\-\-

"You'd better not <u>frighten</u> my grandson!"

_____

_____

\-

_____

\-

_____

The Tub People

Endings -er, -en

Add -er to each underlined word to make a new word.

1. Yuko likes to <u>paint</u> every day.

_____

She is a great _____ .

2. Aldo likes to <u>listen</u> to his sister read.

_____

He is a good _____ .

3. Ashley likes to <u>sing</u> with her friends.

_____

She is a fine _____ .

Add -en to each underlined word to make a new word.

4. The sky is so <u>gold</u> tonight.

_____

Everything has a _____ glow.

5. Did you <u>take</u> my book?

_____

Someone has _____ it.

6. I like my lemonade very <u>sweet</u>.

_____

Please _____ this a little more.

The Tub People

Extra Phonics Practice

Less Common Vowels

Use the words in the box. Write the words to complete each sentence.

| father palm calm put pull full |

_____
- -

1. It was a _____ day
at our home in Florida.

2. I looked at the

_____
- -

_____ tree in
our backyard.

_____
- -

3. It was _____ of coconuts.

_____
- -

4. I helped my _____ pick the fruit.

_____
- -

5. "Be careful not to _____ on the branches,"
my father said.

_____
- -

6. We _____ all the coconuts into a basket.

The Tub People

Phonics Review

G2